ALL THE DAYS OF MY LIFE

RUSSELL J. WYATT

Paperback ISBN: 978-1-944878-62-7

Hardcover ISBN: 978-1-944878-63-4

eBook ISBN: 978-1-944878-64-1

To my children,
to the Third Generation

The Lord is my shepherd;
I shall not want.
He makes me to lie down in green pastures;
He leads me beside the still waters.
He restores my soul;
He leads me in the paths of righteousness
For His name's sake.

Yea, though I walk through the valley of the shadow of death,
I will fear no evil;
For You are with me;
Your rod and Your staff, they comfort me.

You prepare a table before me in the presence of my enemies;
You anoint my head with oil; my cup runs over.
Surely goodness and mercy shall follow me
ALL THE DAYS OF MY LIFE;
And I will dwell in the house of the Lord
Forever.

Psalm 23

FOREWORD

It is an honour to be asked to write the foreword to this book, and more so to have had the privilege of knowing Russell and Anne, and of learning from their many years of experience and wisdom in Zambia. Having met Russell many years ago, I have grown to know him as a man of great stature, not just in his significant height, but as a relatively quiet man of great depth. Russell is well known in farming circles, especially in cattle breeding circles, where he is passionate about the Sussex breed. Russell's influence in church life in Mkushi, and at Chengelo School has been, and continues to be, significant. I am so pleased that he has put pen to paper to record his story for others to read.

This book allows one to share the lives of a couple who have lived for nearly nine decades, and who have been married for over sixty years. In reading it, one becomes acutely aware of some fundamental life principles that when adhered to, help one stand the test of time. As Russell recounts the steps through his life these principles become clear, and those of us who pick them up can learn them from this book, though others of us may choose to learn them the hard way, through the school of hard knocks!

Russell traces his life from early childhood on a farm in the south of England through the difficulties of World War 2; his amazing experiences of moving to Northern Rhodesia all on his own; the challenges he faced working on farms, setting up his own farm as a newly married man, and losing this farm, but not his determination and faith. This bears testimony to the possibility of facing great hardships, but coming out stronger the other end.

Russell and Anne, like all of us, are products of their upbringing, and seldom do we know how profound the influence of our parents is. Both of them, although from two different parts of the world, had the privilege of sound, Godly input in their childhoods. This has had a significant effect on their lives, and gone on to affect the generations to follow them.

Russell and Anne have broken many of the popular rules of seeking wealth, status and recognition. Now, in their late eighties, they have retired. Despite not having a pension they are some of the richest people on this earth as parents to five children, fourteen grandchildren, and twelve great grandchildren, and being thoroughly fulfilled.

Russell has a real gift for writing and an impressive memory for detail that people half his age would be envious of. He has painted a picture that will be passed on to many generations to come. To read this book is to relive the lives of two people in such detail that you almost feel you are on the stage set yourself. Like me, you may find yourself wishing you could have lived in times of old, but as Russell aptly points out in the closing chapters, those days are gone and will never come back. The challenges and joys of life will come in different forms for each of us. The One that will never change is the Father, who has and continues to lead Russell and Anne through their lives.

Peter D. McKenzie de Wet
October, 2017

PREFACE

"Remember all the way which the Lord your God has led you."

Deuteronomy 8:2

Ordinary people usually have ordinary experiences and a normal and unexceptional course unfolds throughout their lives. As a youngster this was what I saw for myself: a predictable lifestyle and course ahead of me, as I anticipated falling into the pattern established by my forefathers. I see now that it does not always work out that way, and certainly did not for me.

Much in my life was, however, quite normal. I grew up and matured, married and had a family, which is now in the fourth generation; I farmed, and now I have grown old, by accepted standards anyway. I have experienced pleasures and achievements, disappointments and failures. Nothing unusual in all that.

Sometimes, though, even a normal life does include some abnormal experiences, and perhaps my life fell into this latter category to some degree. While it is still possible for me to do so, it's good to recall events and doings in one's mind, to trace the way one's life unfolded, and even recount some of the details to others if they are interested; as time moves on, they cannot be repeated.

It may be entertaining to go back over one's past years, but whatever led me to have the audacity to write a book about it? And anyway, who would be remotely interested in reading it?

Everyone of course has a story, some more interesting or exciting, or even more shocking, than others. I could only describe mine as ordinary, although I did stray off the path beaten by my ancestors. I believe some of them did too in their generations by travelling to Australia or North America in the sailing ships of their day. Or so it seemed from the tales my Grandfathers told us when we were small.

More than once folk have said to me in conversation, almost as a throw-away comment,

"You ought to write a book."

Whether this was to slow down my talking, or just as a passing comment, I do not know. Perhaps both. But when a valued and serious friend took the time to call on me one day recently and say as he was leaving,

"I just came to say this. You ought to write a book."

His reasoning, when I questioned him about this ridiculous concept, was,

"Well, you have been around longer than most, and have seen first-hand things that most folk today don't know about or have forgotten."

I could hardly refute that, being in my eighty-ninth year. When I shared this idea with some members of my family, I received only encouragement. So, I had to take it seriously. At the least, it is a retirement project. Hopefully, at the best, it may be of interest to others.

Russell Wyatt,
Kapanda Farm,
Mkushi, Zambia   January 2017

ACKNOWLEDGEMENTS

It is my pleasure to record my sincere thanks to those who gave invaluable help in bringing this project to completion. Without them and their willing efforts this would have never been done. I am most sincerely indebted to them for their considerable input, and in some cases detailed work, as this book is presented first and foremost to my family, and to anyone else who cares to read it. As the recognised Author of this Book there is no way in which I could begin to take all the credit.

Firstly, to my friend Peter de Wet, to whom must go the credit for challenging me to write it, a challenge I could not ignore. Then to the members of my family with whom I shared this bizarre idea, and who encouraged me to give it a go. As the chapters were written they were sent to my daughter, Helen, in Israel and my grandson, Gavin, in Brisbane, Australia, who not only stored them electronically for safe keeping, but read and commented and gave advice as we went. As the project neared completion, they both helped to bring it all together, not the least in selecting photographs from old family albums and hidden in drawers for inclusion.

In the final event there was much family input. Photographic advice and assistance was freely given by our nephew, Gareth Bentley, using his considerable experience and expertise. The photographs that appear on the outside cover of the book were contributed by our granddaughter, Lee. I must also mention our nephew Frank Arthur, as well as Debbie Shapiro in Israel who kindly read through early drafts and gave good advice, and my farmer friend, Mick Marffy, who also read through the first draft and made challenging comments. My thanks to you all.

I would also like to thank the very many folk who have been such a part of my life and my story, making it so full of interest and consequence. Without them all it would have been very dull.

Greatest among these is my wife Anne, whose support throughout our life together, and whose challenging input and enormous contribution, made it all so rich and meaningful.

And, of course our family: children, grandchildren and great grandchildren, a grand total of thirty-one at the time of writing, not to mention their spouses, a further thirteen. To you all I say thank you for your confidence, love and support. On a personal note, I say to you: "Go for it! Never, never, never give up. Life is what you make it, and there are great riches out there just waiting to be explored, experienced, and enjoyed for yourselves."

R.J.W.

1

THE FOUNDATION

"The days of our fathers until now . . ."

Ezra 9:7

"These days should be remembered . . . by every generation . . ."

Esther 9:28

Looking back over the years and the happenings of a longer than average life, I suppose it might and could well have been a very ordinary and predictable one, and certainly different from how it actually turned out to be.

I was born into a West of England family of working farmers with a recorded history stretching back over two hundred and seventy years and no doubt more, and I could easily have stayed in that mould. The norm would have been first to work on my Father's home farm following my school years, and then, with his help, become established on a farm of my own. I would then, no doubt, have married a local farmer's daughter, and together we would have raised a solid family who, in their turn, would follow on in their fore-fathers' footsteps. An expected and approved way of life, which would have been regarded as the right and proper way to go in the community in which I was raised, and the expected pattern for me to follow.

In all this I could have prospered moderately, become a pillar of the local community, a consistent Chapel-goer and supporter, with some shooting and fishing in season for relaxation, respected and secure. We would probably have taken seaside holidays once a year, in between haymaking and corn harvest, and then perhaps in my middle years I would have taken my wife on a daring Continental excursion as a one-off, just to indicate I had made it. Then, at the end of the day, I would have handed it all over to my sons, before being tucked away at a ripe old age in the local Churchyard, gone but not forgotten.

What more could one have wanted? It certainly was the lifestyle and journey of many of my compatriots, school friends, and even some of my family.

The day I left school, everything was on track for my life to be just that. I used to talk it over with my father on exeat weekends from school. But for me it did not happen. So, if not, why not?

* * *

I was born in the year 1927 into our farming family who had migrated eastwards in the early nineteenth century from the county of Somerset and its West Country roots to Sussex in the South of England. I was the fourth child of my parents and the youngest of three boys, with a supporting cast of all four Grandparents living and active, as well as numerous aunts, uncles and cousins. We lived on a medium sized farm on the verge of a spread-out village within five miles of the South Coast.

The family attended the local Free Baptist Chapel in the village; my father was on the Parish Council, and my mother on the District Nurses Committee. Dad was a lay preacher, as was his father, conducting Sunday Evening Services in Village Chapels scattered throughout the county. Apart from that and some very limited social involvements, family life was centred around the farm and its activities. A respectable and respected family in a comfortable but rather circumscribed society which made its way successfully through the inter world wars period.

In writing this account of my life, I must acknowledge the great influence of my forebears in shaping it, even though I slipped out of the mould.

My father's father, Grandpa Wyatt, Richard James Wyatt, the eldest of three brothers, was a Somerset man, as was his father. His speech betrayed that. Grandpa's mother was fifteen when she was married, had three sons before she was twenty and then a daughter, Aunt Kate, twenty years later. In common with many other West Country farmers, all traditional dairy men, he decided to move to Sussex to be nearer the growing milk markets and where farms were larger and land rents were more favourable. He hired a complete railway train and moved his whole family, together with his cattle and horses, farm implements and equipment, to a large farm he rented on the South Downs above Brighton. As I understand it, although he was a skilled and hard-working farmer he was not a good business man. But it was here, on Balmer Farm, Falmer, that he raised his family.

He was a rather flamboyant man who loved to be known as "Farmer Wyatt", and a great talker and raconteur. He raised and ruled his family strictly and even harshly, which did not endear them to him, although they were always loyal. My memory of him was in his retirement, when he and Grandma lived in a cottage near us and looked after some livestock for my father in the little barns and small meadow that were a part of it. Having failed in business, he was supported by his children in his old age. He sported a bushy beard, and appeared very old to us, although he was still quite active. I have heard it said that he should never really have been a farmer but rather a Church Minister, as he had a passion for talking to people about his God, and his heart and joy was in preaching the Word of God.

His wife, Grandma Wyatt, nee Elizabeth Russell Thomas, was the very opposite: a quiet dignified lady, very organised, a loyal wife and loving mother. She came from a Scottish family resident in London and was distantly related to a Scottish aristocratic family. She was a talented artist, and very neat and composed in her appearance.

Although we saw a lot of them and accepted them as part of our family, I realise now that I did not have a close relationship with them at all; in fact, I was rather afraid of them. Perhaps that was my fault, especially with Grandma, as she was loving and had a concern for me, and never forgot my birthday. Although strict and orderly she was kindly and generous and gave us, her grandchildren, little parties. In 1945 she made her first mistake ever over dates, and wrote me a loving letter for my birthday for the third of October, and then passed away quietly and with dignity, as she had lived, before my actual birthday date on the thirtieth. I felt most guilty over my attitude towards her, but it passed, although never forgotten.

My maternal grandparents were quite different. Grandpa Norman had been very successful in business, and retired early to live in some style with our Nana. He employed a groom gardener and kept a good riding horse which he rode to visit us. That was, until he bought a car. He was upright in stature and brisk when he walked, very careful of every detail in his lifestyle, and equally careful with money.

Everything was of value to him. I remember when, having together with my brother delivered some bags of fertiliser to him for his garden, being made to stand amongst his cabbages and brush the fertiliser dust off our clothes for their benefit, while he delivered a little lecture on the evils of waste. When visiting us on the farm one day I saw him collecting hay which had brushed off the hay wagons onto the hedges, and carrying a great armful of it into the barn with the comment, "Enough for one cow for one day".

I learned in time that he had helped many farmers who were in financial trouble during the hard years of the 1930's, not only with loans (which he gave with strict injunctions) but with good, sound advice. He regarded as important every action and decision, and I once heard him say that when young he made a decision to plant a particular crop outside his normal farming practice, the income of which saved him from going under financially.

His beloved wife, daughter of an auctioneer in Yeovil, was to me a very quiet lady, composed and rather withdrawn in some respects, and I never really got to know her as she died when I was still quite young. Grandpa married again and then his troubles seemed to begin. The picture I have of him in my mind is as a tall, dignified and very respectable, but also a rather unhappy man. But I also remember him reading to us with enthusiasm from a book called "Jan Stewer", written in the Somerset dialect that he could reproduce so realistically. It probably reminded him of his own young days in his home setting.

Mum and Dad, as we called them, are very clear in my mind's eye. Perhaps I should talk of my mother first. My memories of her are as a busy and at times rather harassed mother of six, and the wife of a hard-working and committed farmer. She was obviously an excellent manager; meals were substantial and good, and even in the war years when some foods were hard to come by, we always had plenty. And we had hearty appetites.

But I realised in later years that she had not been brought up to this style of life at all. Apparently, her father was rather withdrawn from his family, being taken up with his business, and Nana was rather casual. So, especially in their late teens, she and her brothers and sisters rather ran their own lives.

She and her two sisters were lively young things who lived a joyous life funded by what they could get from their father, who paid up when he had to as a good investment to relieve him of any further responsibility. This changed at the outbreak of war in 1914 when she enrolled as a trainee nurse at a hospital in Southampton, and served there throughout the war. This disciplined training was no doubt a preparation for her marriage to my father and of moving into a very different life style.

Her and Dad's years of courtship were a trial to her, as she had to conform to the strict Wyatt codes of propriety, even though they were both well into their twenties; on one occasion she was "sent home" by Grandma Wyatt for overstepping the mark by staying out on a walk with Dad till after ten o'clock, even though the excuse was that Dad's watch had stopped.

She was a loyal and very supportive wife, and I never heard her complain or compare her role as a working farmer's wife to her earlier years. She was clever and had an excellent memory for detail. This was especially so in regard to family history and connections, and I wish I had listened to her more.

Dad's untimely death after twenty-four years of marriage was devastating for her, and in one sense it was the end, although she lived for another forty years. I never really had a close relationship with her; she was my mother who in my early years directed and controlled much of my life, and although I well remember being spanked by her (she was a whirlwind when roused) there was never a huggy-touchy relationship at all. I think ours was a rather undemonstrative family.

Dad was and still is something of an icon for me. Tall, powerful, a figure of quiet authority, he was fashioned by his upbringing. I find it difficult to do justice to his memory other than to say he was unique to me. I have never met anyone quite like him. He was strong in both body and principles; some would have called him rigid and unbending. He did hold strong views on certain things and from my own standpoint as of now, I am not sure that he was always right. He was a product of his own time and of his upbringing, which could have quite easily made him harsh and unreasonable. But that, he was not.

The prime motivation in his life was, I believe, to honour his God and to care for and provide for his family. In my opinion, he did both. He had a very strong work ethic, with a focus on the broad essentials of his way of life, as well as an attention to every detail in carrying them out. There was a right way and a wrong way to do things, and he knew which was which. But he also had a capacity for fun and enjoyment, and a kindness for others which quietly showed through in his wider relationships.

One of his pleasures was "rough shooting" as it was termed: rabbits, hares and pheasants, and occasionally duck, beating round the hedges and copses on our farm and elsewhere. In doing this he always tried to include others who did not have the same facilities and opportunities that he had.

When he spoke, although in contrast to his father he was a quiet man, people listened. He did not just talk, he had something to say. In action, when there was something that needed doing, he did it, or made sure it was done. It has taken me perhaps a lifetime to appreciate his qualities, which shone through in his everyday life and which I took for granted at the time. He was after all our Dad; we expected nothing less, although we did make fun of him sometimes behind his back.

It is seventy-two years since he passed out of my life. Yet so often, through those years and when faced with a difficult situation, I have thought of him and wondered how he would have handled it. More times than I can say, especially in crises, he has suddenly come into focus in my mind, and I have sorely missed him. "What would Dad have done?"

My life's pathway and involvements would have been totally foreign to him. Nevertheless, the basic principles by which he lived and operated have still applied and been my guide, or at times brought me up short and caused me to reconsider.

Dad was the eldest of a large family, resembling in many ways his beloved mother. His father took him out of school in his early teens and put him into the farm stables as a "carter boy" under the head carter. Early on, he learned to care for and work the huge farm horses that did the heavy farm work, as well as the machinery they pulled—from ploughs to harvesters—doing a man's full day's work. He often fell asleep while kneeling by his bed to say his evening prayers, to be later woken and guided into bed by his mother.

After a year or two of that, he was transferred to the sheep flock, working under the head shepherd, and again learning the crafts and skills of shepherding out on the windswept South Down hills in summer and winter. During the lambing season in January and February he rarely came home, sleeping in the wooden Shepherd's Hut alongside his charges.

His father expected much of him, and was harsh should ever a mistake be made. "Spare the rod and spoil the child" was

Grandpa's view, and one day he went too far. At the age of sixteen, after receiving a thrashing for putting a wheel on the wrong way around on a new machine he was sent to assemble, he stood up to his father and said: "Don't you ever do that to me again!" And he did not. Dad's youngest sister, my Aunty Nellie, told me that from then on, he was recognised as their trusted big brother and their security, and he became a loving support for his mother.

When the first World War started, Dad, with his two younger brothers, walked off the farm and in to Lewis to join the army. Whether this was in a fit of patriotism or to get away from their father, or a bit of both, is hard to tell. Dad and Uncle Walter joined the Sussex Yeomanry, a mounted regiment, and a year later were sent to Gallipoli to fight the Turks.

Being an experienced horseman Dad found himself breaking unruly mules into pack harness on the beaches, before they could be used as transport to carry supplies up the cliffs. He was eventually wounded by a shrapnel burst, and bits of shell case lodged in his leg. He was evacuated and returned to England, but did no active service again. In fact, he was transferred to the Cameron Highlanders, a Scottish Regiment, quite how and why is beyond me. He wore a kilt apparently, and was jokingly called Jock.

He seemed to be able to take a lot of special leave from the army to help Grandpa on the farm, as labour was a problem and Grandpa had a penchant for falling out with his workers. The year after he was wounded, he sheared all his father's sheep with hand clippers, and sowed 200 acres of wheat, broadcasting the seed by hand. This was in spite of his wounded leg and lameness.

He was released from the army in 1918, and returned home. It is astonishing to me that, in a war noted for its massive lists of casualties, my father, his two brothers and their three cousins, as well as my mother's one brother, all returned home safely.

After his release from the army, Dad began to take an increasingly responsible role on the farm near Brighton. Following their marriage, he lived with Mum in a farm cottage and ran the farm for a whole year while Grandpa's tenancy ran out its final course and terminated. Grandpa had finally ceded defeat and moved on to a small poultry farm elsewhere. Mother, who was of course quite partisan as far as Dad was concerned, told me that it was said of Dad by neighbours that had he been in charge all along, it would have been a different story. This was not to be; the stock and implements were sold, and with Grandpa Norman's help, Dad took the tenancy of a small farm on the Hampshire border, which he farmed for a year.

Much of my understanding of this period was from overheard grown-ups' talk. But I heard Dad say once that after a year of his farming there, Grandpa Norman came to visit and walk across the farm, as was his usual habit to see how things were going. After checking the financials, he said to Dad: "You need a better farm than this." And the outcome was that the family moved to Pigeon House Farm: Mum, Dad and two little boys. This became our family home and occupation for the next twenty years, and my own much-loved play-place and later, my work-place.

Grandpa Norman's acquisition of Pigeon House resulted from the financial failure of a large farmer, property owner and horse dealer whom he had tried to help. A document which surfaced in the family solicitor's office when this part of our life was long-gone history, shed some light on all that had transpired. The sad part to me, in putting things together in my mind in later years, was having seen this same large farmer as an old man driving a horse in a County Council rubbish cart around the lanes, a shrivelled old chap with a large hat pulled down over his face and smoking a large pipe, as he held the reins of his ancient steed. A singular lesson of someone who would not, or perhaps could not, move with the times.

At first, my parents had no house to live in at the farm, and for some weeks shared an old army hut up the hill above the village with another young couple and their three small boys. They moved twice to better housing in the village, and then, in the year that I was born, our final home was built on the edge of the farm. This was the home in which I grew up: Pigeon House Farm.

It was built in a part of the very large garden annexed from the Dower House next door. Early photos showed a rather un-developed garden, which Steve, one of the farm workers, slowly brought into order as he could be spared from farm work. There were some lovely old fruit trees in it, which produced the old type of really tasty apples and plums. I have never since tasted anything that comes close to them.

This was my early domain into which I was sent daily to "play". Though what to play at I did not know, especially on my own. Mother was busy indoors with housework and caring for my two little sisters who, at that stage, were house-bound. The outer world for me consisted of the farm, the church across the field where the bells rang out each Sunday and which I could see from my bedroom window, and the village. The latter was to me a remote place of which I only caught a glimpse as I walked to the shop or post office with Mother, or to Chapel on Sundays. It appeared rather dull and uninteresting.

It was the farm which to me was the place of attraction and interest, and as I grew a little older it became the centre of my world. Living things—besides the cat and dogs with which I was already familiar—like sheep, chickens, pigs, cows and the horses lived there, and I longed to make their acquaintance. And there was action there, movement, things happening. Eventually I was allowed outside the gate, a great heavy wooden thing with a nasty catch that held it closed, but over which I learned to climb after I grew too big to crawl through the bars. Now life really started for me.

The late nineteen-twenties and -thirties were known as the depression years. Life was tough, business and farming were tougher. Many apparently well-established farmers failed and lost their farms. Others, who actually owned the land, just lived there and kept a few livestock, doing as much maintenance work as they could and leaving the rest. Some farms became quite unkempt and even derelict. This was low cost, or as it was known "dog-and-stick farming", as they hoped for better times.

Not Dad. First the dairy herd came into being, then a flock of sheep, followed by pigs big and small, and finally free-range poultry; they all came into place and filled and eventually overflowed our farm. And, as I figured later, slotted into the farming pattern. Every day, milk was collected by a great tanker, eggs were sent out twice a week with the carrier in his rickety truck, and pigs were taken to the nearby railway station for dispatch to the bacon factory every fortnight, all with regular efficiency.

It was the constant movement of animals that thrilled me: sheep from field to field, and great pregnant sows brought from the woods and copses where they lived to have their babies in the security of warm, dry pens. The twice daily feeding of the fattening pigs in their special housing, who set up the most uproarious screaming as soon as they heard a bucket rattle, could be heard all over the village. Once the food had been poured out, there was the *slop-slop, mush-mush* as they gobbled it down, and the *swish-swish* as they swept the troughs clean with their snouts for every last drop before waddling back to their sleeping area and settling down again with contented grunts.

Once or twice, I crept into what was known as the piggery while they were all asleep, and rattled a bucket to see what would happen. The result was instantaneous. They woke as one, rushed to their troughs and set up their raucous yelling. There must have been a hundred of them in their various pens, all according to size and age, and their combined vocal effort in their lust for food was alarming. I ran for my life and hid in the feed barn, as I was sure they would eat me given the chance. The noise, in tune but out of time, could not be hid and Dad was not amused, as I learned to my cost.

Eggs were collected every afternoon from the scores of hen houses placed in neat rows across the fields, loaded in baskets onto a cart drawn by Tom, our ancient and steady horse, and brought home where they were graded and packed. Action, action, action; seven days a week.

It was not only the action but also the atmosphere that drew and enveloped me. This was life; things were happening here—the daily routine and yet always something new. The "men" as they were termed, each with their own responsibilities and tasks, moved with purpose and skill to fulfil their part in this on-going round of care and production, input and outcome. And Dad was the planner and director, the one who made things happen, whose word could bring about a change in direction or move things ahead. I followed him around when I could, imitated him, imagined myself, at the ripe age of three and four years, being him and doing what he did so well and with such purpose and calm. This was my world.

Up to the age of five, as I said, this was my world. And I immersed myself in it. The animal smells, the *click-click* of the milking machines, the ewes calling their lambs, the contented grunt of sows feeding their litters, the hens rushing to peck up their corn, the hum of motors on feed-mixing days: this was all music to my ears. How free and lucky I was to be able to roam and become a part of it all.

The men played with me, laughed at me, watched over me, nicknamed me Shep. Even the way they talked—their distinctive Sussex accent, double negatives, drawn out words, and the odd strange unknown words from the past—became my language. My *I's* became *Oi's*, my "*I don't know*" became "*Oi dunno*", which did not please my Mother. And when I came out with some fruity words and expressions at home, I was banned from the farm and gated to the garden for a period. But that did not last. Out there was heaven as far as I was concerned, and myself a free spirit roaming through at will, my imagination unfettered, only showing up at home for meals and sleep, and the enforced cleansing process of a periodic bath.

I had no idea at the time, but this was all too good to last. At about the age of six years I was, to quote one of my great heroes, menaced by education and threatened by the peril of going to school. "Change" became a feature in my life.

2

THE YEARS OF PERIL AND PROGRESS

"I wandered lonely as a cloud
That floats on high o'er vales and hills,
When all at once I saw a crowd,
A host, of golden daffodils;
Beside the lake, beneath the trees,
Fluttering and dancing in the breeze."

by William Wordsworth

My parents' choice of a first school for me was probably a good one, but it was torture for me. The good lady who ran it lived just at the end of the side road that led into the farm, Dairy Lane. It was mornings only at first, but as I sat, or stood, trying to learn or recite dreary and pointless things, I could hear wonderful sounds coming from the farm, just one hundred yards away. Men talking, even shouting, occasionally my Dad's voice clear above the rest, the animal noises, sounds of movement all so familiar and meaningful to me. I could interpret it all in my imagination into the things and happenings of which I, up until now, had been a part. But here I was, caught up in a system over which I had no control and was impotent to oppose, although my parents and other grown-ups seemed to regard it as vital to my well-being.

I could only submit and wait in patience, unresisting, but inwardly in rebellious silence, for the release that came at weekends, and the promised holidays which I was assured would come in time. Surprisingly I did learn some things, and imbibed others subconsciously. I learned to sing "All things bright and beautiful", to repeat the Lord's Prayer (Mrs T. was a faithful attendant at the Anglican Church across the field) and surprisingly, William Wordsworth's poem, "Daffodils".

There were just a very few of us at this school; the eldest was a tall girl with plaited hair hanging down her back, who at the start of every day after Prayers recited this particular poem. After some weeks of hearing this daily I said out loud, "I can say that". I then proceeded to recite it word perfect from beginning to end, to the astonishment of Mrs T. and the annoyance of the tall girl who regarded it as her daily star performance.

How I came to learn it I do not know, I just did. Perhaps it was because I identified with the sentiments of the poet in wandering lonely as a cloud, and being amongst the host of dancing daffodils. Daffodils there were a-plenty in season, growing wild in the Park Land that Dad rented for rough gazing from the Big House on the edge of the farm; loneliness was a familiar experience to me as I wandered solitarily around the farm fields, deep in my own little world. I must have learned how to read and add up, because both took root in my life. Reading opened a whole new world to me, though that was to come in later years, and counting became an obsession. It still is!

However, change eventually came, and I was propelled deeper into the system. I was enrolled in a proper Primary school whose name I still can't spell. This was in our local market town, and each morning I was escorted to the railway station by my older sister, Mary, who was my carer (at the age of twelve) and my loved companion. On the six-minute ride on the train, my brothers being confined to the boys' carriage labelled "Boys only", I was seated among noisy girls in the secluded girls' end carriage, labelled "Girls only". This not only frightened me, but I felt it was an affront to my dignity and status as a boy.

On arrival at our stop, I was handed over to a young lady teacher while Mary went to her school nearby. I was led through the town, along South Street, over a tricky crossing called the Cross, where stood a beautiful Market Cross in this old Roman City, and where there was always a policeman. Finally, in North Street, we climbed some stone steps and passed through a large green door.

The inside was dark and scary, a converted Victorian residence. The school was run by a stout lady who wore woolly dresses and had whiskers. Her staff were delicate young ladies who were terrified of her, as were most of the rest of us. There, for two or maybe three years, I sat at a desk and whiled the time away. Things like arithmetic became more complicated, reading more interesting, geography showed me the wider world which I thought might be worth investigating one day. Biology just seemed to make the simple things of everyday life more complicated and puzzling. Anyway, this period took me through till I reached the great age of nine years, time to move on, and High School became the next stage in my life.

I remember the test I went through to see if I qualified for this next great step in my life: a school of some three hundred and fifty, boys only. I was told to read something out of the book "Black Beauty", about a horse. Familiar ground. But then the examiner, whom I later discovered was the Headmaster (a new breed to me) asked me what I thought were quite pointless questions about what I had read, and which I could only answer with his full prompting. He was certainly, in my view, ignorant about horses. However, I was accepted on this rather shaky basis, and became a fee-paying scholar of the High School establishment, five pounds a term.

I did not do well at High School, in fact even worse than my previous school. Terrible things like physics and chemistry made an entrance to plague my life; French was just learning endless words and verbs of a language which, even after six years of study and learning, I was quite unable to speak. Was that the system, or was it me? All I know was that I got the blame. In Scripture, I thought I knew it all; after all, didn't I go to Sunday School and Chapel? Sports and gym were torture, with a bad-tempered, shouting sports master.

The only relief and joy to me were History and English Literature. I liked the teachers who made it all come alive and encouraged me. What a difference. Gladly, I extended my horizons and entered a wider world through history novels, travel books, and tales of the wilder and developing countries like North America, Australia and Africa, and through some of the old classics about English rural life. So, these were our roots!

I would spend hours on my bed reading and entering into adventures undreamed of, the hardships and exciting experiences of these tough men and women, and the satisfaction of those who overcame. Dad, who was not a great reader himself and who confined himself mostly to the Bible and Pilgrims Progress, did not altogether approve, but he did not interfere. I read under the blanket with a dim torch at night, and hid books under my pillow to grab a moment in the morning.

Before I leave this five-year episode of my life, I must mention people. The Masters, as teachers were then called, varied much from the admired and respected to the hated. "Monkey" Watson, "Fishy" Scales, "Duchy" Holland, "Jammy" Reeves, all different personalities with different styles. The Physics master, with his aggressive and impatient style, closed my mind and understanding to the mysteries of electricity and other like things for ever. The Maths master, by dint of great patience and repetition, showed me that numbers were related to one another. I thank him. The English Literature master exposed the beauty of words and expressions to me, and their ability to project a picture or meaning. I thank him sincerely too.

And then there were the boys I remember clearly: "Coddy" Bland, "Smeller" Marshal, "Tommy" Target whose brother had been in my older brother's class and who was lost at sea soon after leaving school and joining the navy; Ablewhite, who always came first on the class lists as I came last, all because of the spelling of our names. And just plain Wickham, a tubby lad who had lost his father and became my best friend. There were of course many others, lads from all walks of life, those upright and well-mannered, the nasty and bad-mouthed, the fat and useless, the athletic and proud; they were all there, and it was a major part of my education to have to mix and get on with them.

Before I leave the subject of High School, I must mention Thursdays. This was the day of music lessons, conducted by "Percy" Pelham, an eccentric though delightful man no doubt, but whose style was not conducive to our best behaviour. We stood in several ranks around him while he stood, I emphasise stood, at the piano and played with enthusiasm and exaggerated movements, bobbing up and down, bending his knees. We lustily sang our own versions of the songs and melodies he taught us, while pulling exaggerated faces. This he would detect with his musical ear, and in a fury, he would leave the piano without warning and rush through the ranks of boys, scattering them as he went, to seize some poor, selected guy in the back row by the collar and shake him till his teeth rattled. Of course, every boy he had touched or bumped into in his mad rush to get to the victim fell to the ground with exaggerated "OOH Sir's," holding a foot or knee and groaning. It was chaos. Detention was full that night, and we said the Southern Railway had to provide an extra train on Thursday afternoons to cope with those who consequently missed the regular one.

My time there came to an end when my father, who was driving through the town on business one day, saw the School, smart in their green caps and blazers, marching up South Street four abreast on their way to the Cathedral for a special Service. His timing was most unfortunate. It must have been market day too, and in those days livestock were often moved on foot, even through towns. As we marched around the corner so a flock of sheep, plus a man and two dogs, came the other way. Somehow, we became inextricably mixed up, the sheep obviously enjoying the fun and leaping and dashing through our ranks, boys running in all directions, the dogs failing to control either, and the shepherd and master-in-charge completely losing control.

Dad had a front seat view of the whole scene, and as he did have a great sense of quiet humour, must have laughed to himself. But this was not what he wanted for his son. The next day, he gave notice for me to leave school at the end of term. I was thrilled; fate had played into my hands, this was the open door to what I most wanted: to work on the farm. I was fourteen years old, growing fast and developing my strength. Why waste any more time trying to learn useless and irrelevant things when there were more important things to do? Wasn't there a war on, and every man was needed? In my own view I qualified. But little did I know, Dad had other plans.

Seaford College was a Private School that had moved to temporary facilities in a nearby town after its own premises further east had been requisitioned by the War Office for a naval training college. It was there I found myself the following September, a boarder in a school in a South Coast town that was struggling to hold its own in far from ideal premises. Looking back, a long way back, I can see that it was largely due to the boys themselves and the Old Boys Organisation, together with a very sound and strongly entrenched Christian ethic upheld by the Headmaster and one Housemaster, which enabled the school not only to hold on and survive through those difficult years, but to blossom into great things post-war.

But at the time, I was shocked. The first term or two were a difficult time for me: a time of loneliness, of longing for home and my lost freedom, of tears and hiding in quiet spots, as I adjusted to this new way of life. But adjust I did, and I came to realise in time that Dad had made a right decision. This was what I needed. For a start, my self-confidence, which the High School experience had nearly destroyed, took root. I found I could do things which I had been made to feel I could not, and that I was not incompetent or a failure. And more importantly, that I could do well even in an unfamiliar environment. Most important of all, I learned that it was up to me to respond to the opportunities which came my way, and make the best of things even in the most difficult circumstances.

I began to do better in school although I never excelled, and eventually passed the School Certificate with a couple of credits. But it was outside the classroom that I learned the most. The Prefects virtually ran that side of the College, backed by Jiggs the Housemaster. These were boys who, as juniors, had themselves been schooled in the spirit of things by older boys, and were now determined to pass them on. I met boys who had vision, who were bent on developing their own skills, using them, and passing them on. They were not content with the ordinary, but were aiming for the best. It was war time, and they knew they were destined eventually for military service, and even while at school they were planning that, and sitting exams and attending selection boards for specialised commissions or opportunities in the navy and army and so on.

In the College and the House there were rules, not just school rules but entrenched traditions, and failure to observe them brought the wrath of the mighty on one's head. Beds had to be made exactly, with the College Crest on the counterpane in the exact middle. Clothes had to be worn as required, all jacket buttons done up till you had passed School Cert; no hands in trouser pockets either. Surnames only were used, and the Headmaster was the Head, and you knew it. The rules were not enforced, they were observed, and if you did not do so you were way off-line and regarded with disdain. Very effective.

But to go with all this, there was a relaxed comradeship, and help and guidance were given to the uninitiated. The best thing I now realise was that there was an expectation that you could do better than you thought you could, and action was taken on that. This was especially so in sport, and here for me was the greatest change.

First there was rugby, and my first term was rugby term. My introduction was in the front row of the scrum, where my strength was an advantage. I had never handled the funny shaped ball before, but soon got the hang of it. There was no option, I was expected to. Soon the rough and tumble of it all became a joy. I found I was as good as the next, which encouraged me to aspire to the stars. One boy I remember put his shoulder out every time he scored a try, as he fell on the ball, but it never deterred him.

Then there was hockey, at which the school had always excelled. If you played in Seaford Firsts you automatically got a place in the Sussex County team. Although it was the rugby term, the great men at the top were thinking ahead to the Spring term and hockey. The experienced goal keeper had left. What should they do? I and another boy were selected, padded and gloved, and put in between goal posts on the practice pitch one at a time, while the best players pumped the hard balls at us. And they were powerful strikers. I think at first it was to test our nerves, as well as to develop our skills. Anyway, the next term, my second, to my amazement I found myself playing in goal for the school first team. Unbelievable! A scratch team at the best compared with the glorious past, but we held our own, even against adult Hockey Clubs.

I was on my way and for two years and one term, life became not only bearable but really fulfilled as I developed physically and in confidence and ability. I became a regular and enthusiastic sports player for one thing, although never a star. I developed valuable leadership skills, and was finally appointed a College Prefect in my last term, the height of achievement in that environment. Or so it seemed to me. I also made many lasting friends who contributed to my growth. How right Dad had been, and I thank God, even today, for his wisdom and firmness.

Teachers, or masters as they were rightly called, were scarce. The best of them had gone to war. Jiggs was middle aged and unfit, but a first-class Housemaster. He knew when to be angry and exert his authority. When he came into the boys' common room in the evening, every boy stood and silence was complete. Not a move as we waited, expectantly. There might be an outpouring of controlled wrath, or just a quiet, "Carry on boys," as he mixed with his charges. He received utter respect from all.

The "Head" was more remote, a godly man whose Sunday night sermons in the compulsory College Chapel Service were often quoted by the boys, but every bit a Head. We "felt" his presence. He was very musical, and his playing of the Chapel organ was as much an inspiration as his sermons. He had the habit of scratching his nose with his little finger, which every boy in the school could imitate to perfection. It was also the sign that he was around, watch out! These two men, backed by the Prefects, kept the school on track.

Before my last term our Head resigned, and his place was taken by a much younger man, an Old Boy of the school. He was an accomplished athlete, had captained the Cambridge hockey team, and was at that time the British Sprint Champion. It was he who led the College, and I emphasise *led*, after the stringencies of the war years, into one of the best. He is now dead, but I am still a registered Old Boy, although no one there would know me now.

To my astonishment, I was rather sorry when those happy and fulfilling years came to an end. But I was ready to move on. I can still clearly enter into my last school day that late December. With my huge school trunk containing all my school kit, I boarded a train, disembarked at our local station, walked home across the fields, into the kitchen of our house, and said, "I'm home, Mum".

And so began my adult life. After chatting a bit, I asked Mum where Dad was. He was out on the farm, where else? What was he doing? Keeping the work going, with a gang of German prisoners-of-war and the elderly farm workers who were reaping and stacking cattle fodder.

Mum said, "He's not well. I think you should change into working clothes and see if you can help."

I did, and he seemed glad to see me. Having briefly told me what was going on and how to keep it going, and importantly how to maintain the harmony between the farm workers and the prisoners, to my astonishment and dismay he left me to it and went home. I think that was the last work he was ever involved in on the farm.

Christmas came and went, and the traditional Boxing Day rabbit shoot with farming friends took place. I was allowed to shoot in public for the first time, and seemed to do well, which pleased Dad. But during the day he slipped on some ice and damaged his long-standing groin hernia. The next day he went into hospital for an operation.

For the next three weeks I acted as his messenger, running between the two farms and the hospital, telling him what was going on, relaying messages and instructions, cashing cheques and paying wages. I was amazed at his grasp of it all, but also by the confidence he placed in me, and I did my best to respond with real appreciation and effort. He even allowed me to drive his car for doing this, after I had applied for and got a provisional Driving Licence at the County Offices. This was war time, and no time for driving tests. The licence became permanent, and I have never taken a driving test in my life.

All this stretched me to the limit, but I loved it. This was the beginning, I thought, of a really fulfilling life ahead. But that was not to be. Tragedy struck. One Wednesday evening after nearly three weeks in bed, Dad collapsed with a blood clot through his heart, the result of lying still in bed after the simple operation. He fought against it for three days, but on the following Sunday afternoon he quietly surrendered his life.

I will never forget that terrible afternoon, walking from our Uncle's flat over Lloyds Bank in East Street, Chichester, in response to a phone call from the Hospital, up North Street which was slippery with ice and snow, to the Hospital where my Mum and eldest brother were. The distress was heart breaking. I will not dwell on that.

Dad was buried about a week later in our local Church cemetery, in ground he had recently donated for an extension. It was a bitterly cold day. The Service, although in an Anglican Church, was conducted by his closest business friend. He was carried to his grave by his own farm workers, men who respected him and had given him their best over many years. The crowd who came were not only our wide family, but many comrades and friends from his farming and even his army years. There was an

22

atmosphere of stunned disbelief that this powerful, imposing, but quiet, unassuming and steadfast man, was no longer with us. As I heard someone comment, "He was unique".

Things changed dramatically for me from then on. At first, I was still in charge; the momentum Dad had left carried me through for a few weeks, plus the loyalty of the employees to their boss and his farm. But, under the guidance of the Trustees, changes came. My eldest brother sold his small farm nearby and came home with his young wife to manage the farms for my mother. I say this with respect and I hope understanding, but Mum had rather fallen apart after her rock and stay was gone.

I now became just an employee, taking orders as the other workers did, doing the work I loved and enjoyed so much on the farms which had been my life and foundation. But my aspirations and motivation had gone with Dad's death. My brother seemed to expect the same loyalty and interest I had had and would have continued to have had if Dad had been there, but that spark had died too. My second brother was released from the army and was sent home from France to help. He married too and took over the second farm.

As I was now seventeen years old, I had registered for military service as required at that time. However, food was an essential; Britain and Europe were hungry to say the least, and I was in the reserved occupation of food production. I could not even volunteer for anything. I was a fixture. Every three months I received a notice that my military service, to which I longed to escape, was deferred once again. I was restless, even a bit rebellious. Mother had moved to town so my home as I had known it was gone too.

My two elder brothers had taken over the two farms, and I was adrift. Not physically; I was tied down to this essential work, and did feel I was contributing to the war effort and national needs, as was everyone else at that time. But it was in my spirit that I rebelled. My school friends and acquaintances were all in the armed forces around the world. A boy who was junior to me at school won the military medal in Malaya, and here I was shovelling cow dung and sugar beet.

I grew powerful in body as I tried to excel even at that. At first, I worked for one of my brothers, and then the other; no problem in actually doing that, but it was not a happy time. I could not settle, and began to make mistakes and do silly things. The others did their best for me, but Mother was at a loss as she needed to re-align her own life and help my two little sisters.

The straight-forward love and kindness of one of my new sisters-in-law was an anchor for me, and I think she understood. Nonetheless there was only so much she could do beyond feeding my voracious appetite for food. She was a great cook, and understood men must eat. I bought a motor bike, acquired a Border Collie dog and a pretty girl friend, who possibly most fortunately lived far away in Liverpool. To many well-wishers and family, my welfare and future became a matter of concern.

I must say, though, that in many ways those were good years for me. I learned much, greatly enjoyed the farm work and challenges it brought, and took a great interest in all that went on way beyond the actual work. The Young Farmers Club was also an outlet and interest, and I became one of the YFC Cattle Judging team for West Sussex. A great day was the huge YFC Rally, held in the Park of the local Castle. We competed there against five other counties, and I achieved the second highest marks in judging dairy cows, beaten by a girl from Surrey, whom I never met.

It was a glorious day, a wonderful atmosphere; the war was over, there was much fun and attractive side shows. I centered on the corn sheaf pitching competition, a skill I had acquired on the farm even in my school days. Since the age of fifteen I had, together with my school friend Ian, loaded all the wheat, oats and barley grown on our farm in those years, pitching the sheaves up onto wagons for carrying to the great stacks built in the yards. Probably an unknown skill in this present day of combines.

Pitching was not only a test of strength but of skill, and as with all things there was a wrong way and a right way of doing it. With the aid of a long two-tined pitch fork we called a prong, this competition was to propel—or pitch—a sheaf of tightly bound corn over a high bar, much like in a pole-vaulting event.

A massive, tall Canadian soldier was competing against me; probably a farmer from the prairies, he was the base drummer in the Army band who were there as part of the entertainment. Towards evening, only he and I were left, and the bar was raised higher and higher. Who actually won I have forgotten, but I must admit that the sheaf got lighter and lighter as we continually pitched it, and it crashed down to the ground after each attempt.

The long winter of 1946 through 1947 came upon us. Snow was on the ground until March, even in the South of England. Spring was late, and things were slowing down in England; American and Dominion armies had been shipped home, but while the excitement of the war had ceased, the stringencies and shortages continued. It was all a bit dismal. The excitement of Victory Europe, VE Day, had come and gone, and we all wondered what was to come as England and Europe settled down to pick up the pieces and sort itself out. We may have won the war, but the peace seemed heavy going.

Thousands of displaced people from Europe had to be returned and re-established in their home countries, what was left of them. Meantime they were in camps in England. This included many thousands of German POW's shipped from the United States, and being returned home to Germany in stages.

That year, one of my friends and closest companions was a very young German prisoner of war, Fritz, and that really was his name although it was a universal name for them all. While in the transit camp, he was allocated to us for work on our farm, and every day he came and we worked much together. He was a very nice young man, well-mannered and kindly, obviously from a good home, and certainly not the Nazi stereotype we had heard so much of. In fact, in all my contacts with German POW's I don't think I ever met one who was. Often, he missed the truck which came around to pick these men up after their normal working hours on the various farms, as we were still busy, working late. I would drive him home in the evening in an ex-US army Jeep, purchased for fifty pounds at a dump site. I got to know him well, and often wondered how he eventually made out. His home with his parents and younger sister was in what was now the Russian occupied zone of Germany. But at least he had something to look forward to, even if with some trepidation.

It was one day in May of that year that the opening shot was fired that set off a chain of events which totally changed my life and direction. Prior to the war, my parents had befriended and entertained a missionary family from Central Africa. Their daughter, left in England for school when they had returned overseas, had spent some of her summer holidays with us on the farm, and became a friend of my older sister. Now, this couple had come back to England for medical treatment, and my eldest brother met with them again. They enquired of the family, how we had fared during the war years, and how we were coping after my father's passing, asking about each one of us in detail. When I came to know them in later years, I realized what people persons they were.

When they asked about me I have no idea what my brother said. But the response was: "If he is unsettled, what about him going out to my brother in Northern Rhodesia? He is a farmer with a lot of cattle, and he might be able to give him something to do." This my brother passed on to me when he came specially to tell me about it while I was at work. I grasped at this opportunity with both hands. Here was a way out, a way forward. I was open to any suggestion and would have gone anywhere at that stage.

As soon as I could manage, I met up with this missionary myself, travelling to London to visit him in hospital, and chatting with him as he lay in bed. He was an expansive man with a wide outlook; his enthusiasm was contagious, his stories and descriptions vivid, and he really got my attention.

The long and short of it was that I wrote to his brother offering my services, and asking if there truly were opportunities with him if I could get out there. The reply was positive: "Yes, come, there is always something for a young man to do here." Although he gave me to understand that opportunities were there, he did not actually offer me a job. But the opening he gave was enough.

All this was by airmail which seemed good and reliable by the standards of the time, and I replied saying I would like to come.

I waited, and was not disappointed. Soon came the advice on just how to go about it. It was all very optimistic, but then out there they had no knowledge of the restrictions and shortages that we now knew so well. I ignored those, and with great confidence set about getting the ball rolling. After all I was nineteen years old, six feet four inches tall, strong, fit, and in my own view, able and competent. A free agent, no encumbrances. What could hold me back? I grasped the opportunity offered, ignored the difficulties, and set about planning my next move. In doing this I had no idea what the outcome might be. As far as I was concerned, I was on my way.

That was June 1947.

My father, Richard Frank Wyatt

My mother, Dinah Elsie May Wyatt (nee Norman)

Dad as a young man: a skilled horseman and working farmer on the Sussex Downs

The ancient stone Pigeon House (now a listed building), and (in the background) our childhood home built the year I was born. A painting by Anne's Aunt, Kitty Fisher

With my sister Mary; we lived a free and active life

Early days with dogs, cousins, and Roger the horse, all a large part of our lives

The Wyatt Family: three generations at my Grandparents' Golden Wedding, 1942

3

INTO THE UNKNOWN

"Your young men will see visions."

Joel 2:28

The way was now opening before me, and it was just a matter of some action on my part to set things in motion. Or so I thought.

Guidelines set out in an Airmail letter from Northern Rhodesia had been sent to me, received and noted. It was on the basis of these that I now took action.

First, so I was advised, contact The Union Castle Shipping Line and book a one-way passage to Cape Town. This I did, no problem, but the reply was shattering. They might just as well have said, "You must be joking", though were too polite to do so. The war was over, and thousands of people were trying to get back to their home countries around the world after war service in Europe. English brides were trying to follow their colonial husbands, while others were looking for a new life in brighter climates. Maybe in a year, maybe two; they had put my name on the list. Glad to be of service, yours faithfully, etc., etc.

However, they had made the mistake of including their phone number on the letterhead. Nothing ventured, nothing gained, I thought, so I phoned. As luck would have it, or was it more than that, a kindly and sympathetic man answered the phone. Bless him. I stated my case. I wanted to go now, I said, if not sooner, and any delay would be of no interest to me. The man was not only sympathetic but also patient and understanding.

"Now listen carefully," he said. "I have a proposal to make."

I did! He confided in me that if I was prepared to sail at forty-eight hours' notice, he might just be able to get me a booking.

"Absolutely no problem at all!" I responded, although I did not tell Mum.

In the end, it turned out to be ten days. They found me a booking on the Carnarvon Castle liner, to sail in early September. That was in the year 1947.

The second guideline was on how to equip myself, and for that I put myself in the hands of a company in London that I had been told specialised in equipping people for life overseas in remote areas. At least so they said, but amongst a number of other useless things they sold me, I did acquire a useful Tilley pressure gas lamp, an essential mosquito net, and a most unsuitable P14 .303 match rifle. The London Company agreed to pack all this in a trunk, marked with my name, and dispatch it to Southampton to be stowed below as cargo in the ship on which I was to sail.

"This is our business," they said, "and here is the account!"

I then applied myself to more personal things. There was my loved Border Collie, for whom I found a home and a new working life on a sheep farm on the Sussex Downs. My motorbike went too, and I sorted and packed my few belongings. My little girl friend had gone to the United States with her parents, so that was no problem. I was presented with a watch, a camera, and a writing case (hint, hint) by my family, and I was ready to leave my old life behind and go.

The last week or so I spent travelling around to say goodbye to the wider family, which included a wonderful day rabbit shooting with Uncle Moorely Goodwin, a bluff and cheery Somerset farmer of the old school who was married to my Dad's young aunt, Aunt Kate. I don't think he was much shake as a farmer, but he was great fun to be with.

I must mention my Mother. She was wonderful, and never stood in my way, although I think she was sad. She possessed an adventurous spirit, and having lived a fairly circumscribed life herself, she was perhaps a little envious.

My last day I spent on the home farm, now run by my eldest brother, feeding sheaves of barley into the great threshing drum surrounded by the constant loud drumming of the great machine and enveloped in dust, as we threshed out that year's harvest. That was the sort of skilled and demanding job which I enjoyed, although it was usually reserved for older and more experienced men.

The next day, accompanied by Mum and some of the family, my brother drove us to Southampton, and I was delivered to the shipping line offices, from where I was directed on board. There was now no turning back.

* * *

The *Carnarvon Castle*—one of the Union Castle Lines' great steamer liners which plied the South Africa route—had had its own war experiences. Years later, I met a man who had served on her when she had been operating as a sort of armed fighting vessel. She had been badly mauled in a battle encounter for which she was barely equipped, following which, when repaired and converted, she became a troop carrier. This was what she was when I came on board. She had not been upgraded to suit civilian use; the need to shift people around the world was too great and too urgent.

We left Southampton and sailed that night with around thirteen hundred people, besides crew, on board—men below decks, women and children in officers' quarters—all a tight, even cramped, fit. My sleeping quarters were on the bottom bed of a two-inch piping framework, five beds high, which seemed to stretch the full length of the ship's hold. I slept back to back against another man, with just a flimsy division of hessian sacking between us, and whom I never got to know. Fortunately, he was a quiet sleeper.

Lying in my bunk, I could see through a tiny porthole, and watch the sea waves rising and falling. By day two, crossing the Bay of Biscay, I was sick as a dog. But it passed, and once I'd found my "sea legs" I began to explore my surroundings.

To describe my fellow passengers as a mixed bag would be reasonably accurate. There were all sorts: tough ex-service men and women who had experienced some rough years of war, escapees from a rather dismal post-war England (was I one of them?), some looking for a new life, others on their way back to their homes to resume a previous life that had been rudely interrupted five years earlier. They were all there. A tall, blond "Mr. Universe" type, acutely aware of his stature and dramatic appearance as he strutted around followed by a group of infatuated girls, soon found his match in some tough, war-hardened albeit shorter men.

We made a brief call at Madeira, anchoring in a bay off the island. That afternoon, many folks went ashore for an hour or two, while shady characters in small boats came aboard offering their wares for sale, ranging from dubious trophies and nasty postcards to their "beautiful sisters". Mum would have been horrified, but a lot of it went over my head.

Quantities of Madeira wine came on board that night. Once the ship was under way again some Scottish ex-soldiers donned their kilts and got out their swords and bagpipes, the result of which was my sole experience of an uninhibited Sword Dance performed with a wildness straight out of their Highland past. We sailed off into the darkening sky for the longer stretch of our journey, while the bagpipes played all night in our confined quarters below decks. This was a very different world to the orderly home I had left behind in England.

By some chance, I was befriended by a mixed group of folk. Every day, we would sit on deck in the sun and just while away the time. Among them was a young English lady on her way to join her South African husband who had already been flown home after his war service in Europe. I owe much to her. I think, in retrospect, that she spotted my naivety and kindly befriended and shielded me in the most unobtrusive way. Looking back, I realised there were the ingredients on that ship for going seriously wrong and getting into really bad company. By the grace of God and her friendship, I escaped that.

One morning, after thirteen days at sea, we woke to an unusual stillness, no rumble of engines or rocking movement. And there, not so far away, was Table Mountain. We had arrived, and what followed was a long day.

The South African officials came on board; they seemed very wary and careful as they screened us all. With good reason, I think. I produced my "letter" from Mr Fisher and was told I was not to stay in Cape Town but to catch that night's mail train for the Rhodesia's. I think some people found themselves in detention or holding camps until their futures were clearer to the authorities.

Arrangements had been made through friends back home for some of their South African family to meet me off the boat. This they did and after taking me to their home, they saw me onto the train that evening, complete with a basket of local fruit. I was off into the depths of Africa and my unknown future with nothing but a handful of carry-on luggage, my trunk from the ship's hold having temporarily escaped me.

After a night in the narrow top bunk of a shared compartment, sleepily aware of the train's movement and *clacketty-clack* of the wheels on rails, I woke to bright sunlight and clear skies, and the landscape of the Karoo, so very new to me, but so fascinating. I watched the passing sheep farms, vehicles racing along dirt roads beside the rail tracks, trailed by clouds of dust rising high into the sky, and African women and small children, all selling strange things or asking for money alongside the train whenever and wherever we stopped. There was a leisureliness about our train journey, so unlike the Southern Railways of my youth that ran to the strictest timing. We stopped at one station where there was even a dance floor and music, and people disembarked from different stationary trains and danced together until their respective trains whistled their intention to move on.

My companions in the sleeping compartment were an artisan from the North of England who had been in the Parachute Regiment and had parachuted down into the battle of Arnhem, and a rather nasty little man with a mind to match who hoped to get a job in Southern Rhodesia. He did not seem a likely proposition to me. We were joined for one day by an Afrikaans railway employee, my first experience of this fascinating race, who asked in faltering English what language the North Country Englishman was speaking.

At Bulawayo, it was a change of trains and a move into yet another new world. Quiet, well ordered and confident, we proceeded on, over the Victoria Falls and into the North. I met people on this train who knew the Fisher Family, and introduced me to my new world, which seemed at the same time vast yet in some ways smaller, where everyone knew everyone else. The food in the dining cars fulfilled all I could desire in quality and quantity. As I was fairly hefty and well built, someone commented that I was a poor advertisement for starving Europe.

Then, at the end of this five-day train journey, so different from my initial six-minute journeys to school, I stepped off the train, according to my guiding instructions, and onto Northern Rhodesian soil at Kitwe. A little at sea, I looked around, wondering what my next step would be. My guidelines had now run out.

I need not have worried. There to meet me were two friendly and obviously responsible middle-aged ladies. Apparently, in this country there was a community spirit which made it quite normal to ask for help or services of friends and acquaintances, and these, if at all possible, were willingly given. These ladies, one a Missionary and the other a Government District Nursing Sister, had been asked to meet this young newcomer, look after him, and see him on his way.

They were kindness itself, and I later came to know them well. I stayed with them for three days, and they gently initiated me into a few of the ways of this new world. They quietly researched my background and what sort of a chap I was. But one question was crucial: did I have any sisters? Yes, I had three. I was astonished at the apparent relief on their faces.

"Well," they explained, "there are several girls in the Fisher family where you are going, but you will be used to that."

Little did they know. But that was to come.

Three days later, I was taken to a transport depot outside Kitwe where I boarded a bus. At least that is what it was called; it even had the grand name of "Mail Bus". Armed with some sandwiches and drink, I climbed in, farewells were waved, and away we went.

To call it a bus was indeed a stretch of the imagination, so far removed was it from our local Southdown Buses back home, or even the old Silver Queen, nicknamed the Old Grey Mare, which slowly plied its way daily between the local towns there. This vehicle was an adapted small truck with a box body on the rear. The door was at the back, and inside were the so-called seats, consisting of benches made of half-inch tubing spaced a hands-breadth apart and stretching the length of the truck body. There was no back rest. However, it was crammed with cheerful and chattering people and their luggage, all set for the day's adventure.

I was ushered into the front seat beside the driver, a smartly dressed young man, but not a communicator. No one spoke to me (maybe they could not speak English) but they treated this tall, strange young man in unsuitable clothes with heavy glasses and long, bushy hair, which was me, with respect but also probably with wonder and amusement as well. For six or seven hours we bumped along the rough, winding and dusty road in complete silence, apart from the racket of the much-shaken bus. There was little to see apart from endless trees, and one or two small streams, and enormous mounds of earth, which were anthills, as I was later informed.

Finally, the truck groaned its way up a steep hill, turned off in front of a barn-like structure, the only building we had seen all day, and stopped. The cheerful folk in the back all bailed out and disappeared, as did the driver. I was left alone. Not a word was spoken to me. So, I too disembarked, and went and sat on some sacks in the barn to await events.

Half an hour or so later, I spotted a man coming towards me. He was dressed in an immaculate white uniform with a white cap jauntily placed on one side of his head. He was carrying on the fingertips of one hand a tea tray in waiter style, all nicely arranged with tea pot, milk jug, cup and saucer.

"Good morning, Sah," he said, although it was mid-afternoon by now. "Some tea," and he put the tray down on a nearby fuel drum and disappeared.

I was ready for a good cup of tea after the dusty ride. When I had finished, the man returned, his timing perfect, and politely carried off the tray. Then another wait, as I wondered what unexpected thing would happen next. Would I spend the night here? Would someone suddenly produce a bed? Anything was possible, so it seemed. What did happen next was as unexpected as everything else, and it opened the next door to my new life.

After an hour or two I heard the rumble of a car engine far away in the silence of this place, which became progressively nearer and louder. Then around the corner and into the yard, accompanied by the inevitable cloud of dust, came a large, blue American Ford Mercury car. It stopped, the dust settled, and out stepped a middle-aged man dressed in khaki tunic and trousers. He limped around the car towards me.

"Hello, you must be Wyatt," he said in a clipped, army officer-type voice, "I am ffolliott Fisher. Well done, you have got this far. I have come to see where you had got to."

I had met the man who was to be first my employer, then my guide and helper, my friend and a massive influence on my life, and eventually my father-in-law. A man for whom I still have an immense respect. That he had driven two hundred miles to find me escaped me at the time.

"Bring your kit. Put it in here," he said as he opened the enormous boot of the car.

We got in, the car started with a roar, and once more we were on the road. After about twenty miles, we turned off up a small track into what turned out to be a Mission Station and Mr Fisher pulled up outside a large thatched house.

"We spend the night here," he said.

Although they had not been expecting us, the lovely American couple whose home it was made us very welcome. Once again, I experienced the extraordinary hospitality of this country.

The final stage of my three-week journey began at about five the next morning, and was an experience that I have repeated scores of times since. We pulled away from the house in the fading darkness and out onto the bush road. Down into a valley we drove, over a bridge, and up the steep hill turning right at the top. This was the only turning where it was possible to go wrong for one hundred miles in either direction. No sign posts, but if you did make a mistake, you would travel for half a day or more before you found out. Then we followed the same dusty, winding road through endless tree cover, interspersed with the enormous anthill mounds. Occasionally, we crossed a small stream, and once or twice a larger river.

It was at one of the streams that we stopped for mid-morning brunch; a new concept to me, two meals in one. The African man accompanying us knew the routine and soon had a wood fire going. In fact, two. Over one fire he boiled a pot of water and made his own food, a sort of stiff porridge called "*nshima*". The other fire he spread a bit, placing a kettle for tea at one end while Mr Fisher, using a blackened old frying pan, fried eggs and bacon at the other end. All these supplies had been stored in the food box in the boot of the car, an essential item for long distance travel. It was a slick operation, and in less than an hour, refreshed by the food, a "convenience" trip into the seclusion of the bush and a wash in the stream, we were on the road again.

As we journeyed through midday we saw very few people, one or two small groups of thatched mud and wattle huts, and gardens or small fields growing rather sad looking crops of some kind. About this time, we passed a man who, supporting himself upright with the aid of two sticks, was dragging himself along the road. A woman with a small child on her back walked slowly and patiently beside him. Mr Fisher pulled up, and a conversation took place in a language I could not understand. The outcome was that the man accompanying us moved up, the crippled traveller and his wife were helped into the back seat of the car, and we proceeded on our way.

Mr Fisher told me that this man had been employed on the mines near Kitwe. He had contracted what appeared to be polio, and instead of going to the Mine or Government Hospital facilities right there in the town, where he could have been helped, he decided to return to his village over three hundred miles away. Having insufficient money for the bus fare, they set out walking. How long he had been on the road I cannot imagine, but as far as I could make out he had struggled along, covering in this way at least two hundred miles. To my mind, it was crazy, although heroic. He was thin, dressed in rags, and exhausted. His wife wore that patient but dull look of fatalism recognizable among these people at times of stress, which in time I came to know better.

It soon became obvious that washing had not been a part of the man's recent actions. However, we pushed on, and eventually crossed a very wide river by way of a wooden bridge that rattled and banged as we crossed, and up a hill into a small town. This was termed the *Boma*, the District Headquarters of a huge area called Mwinilunga. Here, our passengers remained to be taken in to the local Government hospital care. We were now within fifty miles of our destination.

Before we left, Mr Fisher stopped in front of a small country store on the edge of the town, out of which emerged a tall and dignified-looking man to greet him, Mr Munjunga Downes. He was the man in charge of this outpost trading store belonging to the Fisher Company. A long conversation in the local language ensued. As Mr Fisher talked, Mr Downes would say now and again what sounded to me like "Aaamen". However, I learned later that it was a very polite response of agreement and understanding, "*Enga mwani*".

As we drove, the road became narrower and more overgrown the further we went, winding through heavy bush country with which I was to become so familiar. Crossing over a couple of rivers and streams of clear, sparkling water, we finally came into more open country as the car went slowly down a steep hill towards another river. There on our left was a large herd of red cows and calves pouring out of the bush, across open ground, splashing through the river and up the other side. It was for me the first glimpse of what was to become a major part of my life: cattle farming in Central Africa.

Minutes later, we drew up in front of neat stone steps leading up to a large and beautiful thatched house surrounded by open space and lovely gardens. I had reached my destination at last and without a hitch, and here I was kindly welcomed into the Fisher Family.

It was to become my new home for the next two and a half years, and the launching pad for the rest of my life. It remains today as beautiful as ever in appearance, but also as a centre and anchor of the family life of which I eventually became a part.

4

THE WAR, 1939 TO 1945

"A time of war, and a time of peace."

Ecclesiastes 3:8

Before I leave Europe and England completely behind me in the course of my journey, a huge chunk of my story would be left out if I did not include the five years of WW2, including its run-up and a bit of the aftermath. Those years were formative ones for me, not only as a period of growing up through teenage years, but in encompassing a unique experience that had a profound effect upon me. Even now, so many years later, the memory and impact of it all is of great significance to me.

As the late 1930's were coming to an end and I was moving towards my teens, I was aware that trouble was brewing. A little man with an outsize moustache and in need of a haircut, together with his "gang" in Germany had become something of a joke to many ordinary folk. As boys we imitated his strutting walk, his special salute, his *Heil Hitler!* greetings, his moustache and hair style. Even a comedy film was made in America about him, starring the comedian Charlie Chaplin, and called "The Great

Dictator". But gradually, the comedy faded and the realization dawned that this was no joke, but a serious threat.

With that realization, a cloud of deep concern settled over our communities. The memory and horror of WW1 was very real to middle aged folk like my Dad. A repetition was unthinkable. Dad brushed it off a bit when I asked him one day what war was like, as I was riding with him in the car. Maybe he did not want to scare me, but it left me uncertain as to what to expect, in between my boredom at school and my busy life on the farm.

The reality came one Sunday morning as we were sitting in Church, when I heard for the first time the wailing of air raid sirens which truly gave me goose bumps, and to which we were soon to become accustomed. The war had started. A number of men got up from their seats and silently left. The rest of the congregation sat pale and still, with only the sound of a few stifled sobs here and there.

However, after that frightening start, the next few months seemed a bit of an anti-climax, almost disappointing to a young boy who was expecting action. The British army was sent to France, we knew that. Photographic shots in the weekly Picture Post news magazine showed soldiers celebrating Christmas in the snow, in the fields and trenches. Tame stuff. Apart from that nothing beyond a little air activity.

Life went on as usual, apart from army units moving about the country in training. They dug trenches here and there, set up strong points, and on one occasion, drove their vehicles across our farm, leaving gates open so the dairy cows strayed all over the place, and wheel tracks across our fields of wheat and oats. The young officers, wearing very new uniforms and a new authority, were surprised when Dad made a few suitable comments to them.

Then, in May 1940 things started to happen. At first, I did not grasp what was really happening at all, but Dad and my older brothers were listening to the radio and reading the Daily Telegraph at every opportunity to follow what was going on in France, Holland and Belgium. Obviously, it was causing concern.

The happenings of the next few years have been well recorded, but to us on the ground of the South Coast of England, what we saw was real, first-hand stuff, and scary. Dunkirk, never heard of before by most folk, became a part of everyday conversation. Boats were required—any number, any size—to bring our army home. We could not help in that. We were farmers, landsmen.

Then soldiers began to appear in our village, young men with tired faces and worn uniforms, relieved no doubt to be on home ground but probably as bewildered as we were. A unit of the Royal Artillery moved into the Big House on the edge of the farm that had been unoccupied for years. They were issued with ancient six-inch guns, which they installed under the trees in the Park and trained on the mouth of the river, five miles or so away. To Dad's fury, they camouflaged the guns with branches from trees they had cut down in the Big House gardens, including the Yew Tree which was tasty to cattle but deadly poisonous, and five of our heifers ate it and died.

These men of the Royal Artillery were mostly from North Wales; many hardly spoke any English, but could they sing! Each week night, they gathered in the local Pub and sang the grand old hymns that they had sung at home. On Sunday evenings they piled into the Village Chapel and sang the same hymns, in Welsh of course, to the consternation of the local Sussex folk. Dad and Mum welcomed some of them into our home over the weekends for meals, but conversation was stilted. They talked little of their recent experiences except the funny bits, which were few and far between.

One man had managed to get off the Dunkirk beach and on to a Destroyer. He had not shaved for two weeks, he said, and decided to tidy himself up a bit, as a good soldier should. He was half way through his ablutions when the Destroyer was attacked from the air. That was the end of his clean-up operation, and he landed on the South Coast with a hefty black beard on one side of his face and clean shaven on the other.

After a short lull, things started to happen again in that August of 1940, this time right above us. One day, as we worked in the farm yard in preparation for our first war-time harvest, we saw a group of enemy aircraft flying in formation, passing right over us and heading inland, high in the clear blue sky. White puff balls of bursting anti-aircraft shells appeared all around them, and they turned back to fly away over the sea. For us, these were the opening shots in a battle that was to last for weeks.

The next Sunday, August 4th, I was at a friend's house looking out from an upstairs window to see what we could as the air-raid sirens were wailing. It turned out to be a front seat view. Two groups of enemy aircraft were flying in from the sea, quite low, and as they came over the near-by air base they peeled over, one by one, screaming down in a steep dive onto their target, releasing strings of bombs as they went.

For the next hour, the frantic noise of earth-shaking explosions and the roar of aircraft diving and climbing deafened us. We ran downstairs and into the safety of the underground shelter in the garden. I would have loved to have watched the ensuing air battle, as British fighters came down like a pack of wolves on their prey but it was too dangerous, as much of it was at little more than tree-top height. The Stuka bombers, helpless against these fighter planes, scattered and raced in all directions, like rats running from terriers, trying to escape the vicious and determined fighter pilots. Few of them did. These men were out for revenge against an enemy who for the last few weeks had had it all their own way across Europe.

Eventually the noise subsided and nervously we crept out of the shelter into a now darkened scene. The glorious summer sky was gone as heavy black smoke from the fuel and ammunition stores blew eastward over us and obliterated the sun. So much damage had been done. Every now and again a fighter plane cruised around above us, like a terrier dog sniffing the ground, just in case some enemy craft had escaped them and was still lurking.

Years later, as I walked around the burial ground in a Churchyard near that air-base, I saw a long row of head stones bearing the names of young girls and their service ranks, all in their early twenties, who had been killed on that day. My mind went back to that afternoon, and I was sad for those girls. I could just picture them in their bright uniforms, laughing and full of fun as together they enjoyed this new experience in the Airforce, as we had seen them so often. And then suddenly, to be wiped out that glorious summer afternoon.

From that day on, the Battle of Britain, fought overhead in the skies across Southern England, was a daily thing. Each evening, we listened to the radio for the latest news of the battle, and to hear the "score" of enemy aircraft destroyed, and the numbers of ours lost in the battle. Almost every day for the next few weeks we saw action, sometimes very high in the sky, and heard the faint roar of engines and the rattle of machine guns as the airmen fought it out. Occasionally, there were faint explosions and flashes of light, followed by parachutes quietly floating down. Now we knew there was a war on.

From September, this battle gradually diminished, and the days grew quieter as it became mostly night flying. I would lie in bed in the darkness listening as enemy bombers groaned their way overhead, like heavily loaded lorries, on their way to decimate our big cities. Night raids were made on Portsmouth; we could see the action in the distance, and the glow of fires caused by the raid. Fighter plane bases in our area were attacked too. Occasional explosions in the distance and flashes of light through the curtains kept me awake.

One night, there was an explosion that shook our house, causing something to fall off the wall above my bed and on to me, frightening the life out of me. Dad had built a very solid air raid shelter in the garden, with little benches and shelves, and concrete seats around the walls. Not knowing what to expect, Mum had stocked it with survival food, secreted on the higher shelves, there for use in case we would have to take cover for long periods. The door had to be kept locked against raids by myself and my little sisters on the emergency food supplies. The temptation and the expectation were there, along with pleading for just a taste.

"No, those are for when there is an air raid."

It had to come.

The wailing sound from the local town carried through the night for miles around. That was the much-awaited signal. With incredible speed, my two little sisters had rushed out of bed, down the stairs, through the garden and into the shelter, unlocked just in time by Dad to let them in. With complacent and expectant faces, they sat themselves down on the cold bench.

"Now can we have some chocolate?"

A darkness seemed to descend over the land as we settled into this stage of the war routine. Shining through this darkness, however, was a tremendous sense of purpose as we were inspired by the great leader who emerged onto the public scene, speaking in his growly voice to and for the nation.

Bad news there was a-plenty. Cities were decimated, countries lost to the enemy far and near, ships sunk, men and women killed. At school, every Friday the Headmaster read out a list of Old Boys—past pupils—who had been killed in the fighting that week; some had been Fighter Pilots, killed while defending their own home countryside. Some older brothers of my own class mates were among them.

We soldiered on through that winter and into another spring and then summer. But change was coming. The nation was being mobilised and geared into a great force of confident people, determined to do their part (whatever that might mean) in order to overcome the terrible threat that had subdued so many around the world. The mood was infectious, and I caught it. It never occurred to me that at the end of the day we would not overcome and win. After all we were British, and this was the British Empire! Extreme nationalism I suppose, but it carried us through.

We saved for victory, we dug for victory, we worked at anything we could do to help the War Effort. Cars were immobilised (so they couldn't be taken and used by German airborne troops if and when they landed), road signs removed, obstructions raised in the fields, and movement of people restricted. The Local

Defence Volunteers (LDV), later to become the Home Guard, was formed. About one hundred men of all ages, from teenage boys to fifty-year-old men, formed our local platoon. Dad was one of them, and the sole armour of these men for a start were two twelve-bore shotguns and five No. 5 cartridges, which Dad used to shoot rabbits.

Invasion was expected at any time as the German army, navy and air forces gathered their strength only forty or so miles away across the English Channel, ready to invade and subdue our country. False alarms were many, and one evening the phone rang. The rather pedantic voice of the local commander, a WW1 veteran who had lost one eye, transmitted clearly into our sitting room.

"Mr. Wyatt, I wonder if you would mind coming round. And bring your gun. They are on the way."

A call to mobilisation! Dad came home just before dawn, an anti-climax, but a relief nevertheless.

On the farm, huge changes had to be made as part of that great national mobilisation. The nation had to be fed; a diet and menu had been worked out, and British farms had to produce the goods. This project was overseen by Lord Woolton who, I believe, started life as an office boy in the general store, Lewis and Co., and rose to be its Chairman. The poultry and pigs had to go, and the sheep too, much to my sorrow, as there was no food or room for them on our fertile land. Across England, sheep were consigned to the un-ploughable hills and mountains; pigs became rare, and everyone was encouraged to keep a few hens in their back gardens and feed them on scraps for the odd egg. In their place on our farm, fields that had once been pasture were ploughed up and planted with potatoes, sugar beet, and wheat, as well as fodder crops for the dairy herd.

We had new and unfamiliar machines to operate and had to learn new skills. The skills that Dad and the other middle-aged workers had used in their youth were now revived and came in to full play, harnessed for the war effort.

When the time for the first wheat harvest came, Dad said to

me, "You are too young to do a man's work; you'll have to drive the tractor which pulls the harvest binder."

At my protest, he said, "You will learn as you go, and I will be behind you."

He was, and I did. I was twelve years old. In fact, I prided myself that I became quite an expert at the job as we worked on, day after day, even if only in my own eyes. Dad never complained or scolded, just guided. To run over and flatten a few stalks of wheat with the tractor wheels as I turned too sharply at corners was so much food lost, and just not done. So much for child labour—I'm all for it in that kind of positive and educational form.

When I was fifteen, Dad reversed things. I was now tall and strong, and able to learn a man's work. The local shoemaker with a crippled leg now drove the tractor, doing his bit for the war service. For the next three years, together with my school friend Ian, we "pitched" all the corn harvest. In laymen's terms, this meant throwing or passing the corn sheaves from their stooks— where they had been standing on end in the field to dry out for a couple of weeks after cutting—up and on to wagons. When fully loaded, the wagons were hauled away by a tractor driven by a young boy or girl, and the sheaves stacked in "ricks" to await threshing out in the coming winter. Placing the sheaves in order and loading the wagons ten feet high was done by "Land Girls", also doing their war service, but who were usually novices at the job. It had to be done correctly or the load would slide and fall off en route to the ricks.

We were proud of our job and of the skills we acquired as we went. And we had a lot of fun. I remember one clear and sunny day, however, when an enemy aircraft flew in low from the sea and circled round us. We dived for cover under the wagon expecting a burst of machine gun fire directed at us to erupt any minute. Luckily for us, a couple of enthusiastic Hurricane fighters appeared over the hedges ready for the kill, and the intruder fled for home.

There were other incidents that were very close to home, some shattering and terrible. An Aunt and Uncle were wiped out when their house took a full blast from a lone bomb on the outskirts of London. An enemy bomber blew up one night right over the village when it was caught unawares by a night fighter, and the pilot came down in our garden, his parachute draped over the huge walnut tree. There is a photo of that somewhere. Dad "captured" him, brought him indoors, and Mother made him a cup of tea. What else when someone comes to visit unexpectedly? It was three o'clock in the morning. He was the perfect gentleman, and bowed and clicked his heels when he left, escorted by our local policeman. His war was over. Just an hour or two earlier, he had been up in the sky on his way to bomb the hell out of one of our cities. Puzzling. I wonder what he made of the kindly English family who made him welcome in the middle of the night.

We often had soldiers and air force men and women come to our house. They were far from home, and a little lost at this turn of events in their lives. Among them were some Canadians, a tough but friendly bunch who loved helping on the farm when they could get away from their camp.

One man I remember well, a farm lad from the Prairies, who often came to our home. He was part of the Field Ambulance Corp, an incredibly brave bunch of men who moved unarmed in battle with the front-line fighters, helping the wounded of either side wherever they could. I clearly recall seeing him one day, walking up the driveway to our house, slowly and it seemed to me in a daze, so different from his usual cheerful self. He confided later to my parents that he had spent the previous week or so cleaning the blood and gore out of landing barges and small boats, and burying his fellow soldiers who had been killed right there in the vessels before they could even reach land. It was the tragedy of a commando raid gone wrong.

Friends from London also came to stay, shattered by the constant air raids and gunfire, and in desperate need of just nothing more than sleep and quiet. This was indeed a "Peoples War", in which we were all involved in one way or another.

At home, there were changes too. Maps appeared on the walls so we could follow events, along with outline diagrams of different types of aircraft so we could learn to identify enemy craft from our own. Blackout curtains, horrible black things, had to be drawn over windows each evening before lights were switched on, so as to prevent even a chink of light showing outside.

Food was a big item throughout the war, and some folk really battled. But my Mum was a very good manager, and she had laid in stocks of tea and sugar when there was still plenty. These were handy for Christmas presents too when there was not much else, and always gratefully received. We were never hungry, although some of the dishes we ate were made up of grated vegetables, cheese and anything else going, and were never given a name. Mum did her cooking "out of her head".

Every bit of fruit and veg in our garden was preserved, and there was endless bottling and jam-making in the late summer months. Ration cards were the order of the day, and meat scarce. Rabbits shot at harvest time and in the winter helped. A few hens still survived; fed on scraps they provided us with eggs.

Our daily breakfast of bacon and eggs continued; not even Hitler was allowed to interfere with that. And, joy of joys, we were allowed to fatten one pig a year, or was it two? A permit had to be acquired and bacon coupons surrendered. This was a challenge to which Dad rose with his boyish sense of humour. The size of the pig was not stipulated in the permit; it was fed on food waste from the local army camp, which I collected each Saturday in an old horse and cart. The happy chap grew to an enormous size and, when the time came the door had to be removed and some of the wall too, in order to get the unfortunate animal out of its pen. The result were the most enormous hams which Dad cured in salt brine in a half tub, faithfully rubbing and turning them each evening.

Clothes were on ration too, which was particularly problematic for me as I grew at an alarming rate. Shoes were replaced when they were worn out, not when they became too small for my feet. I have had crooked toes all my life to bear witness to that, my own type of war wounds and evidence of my contribution to the War Effort.

But—and I must add this—it became a matter of pride to make do, to have no sugar in our tea (that was kept for the jam), to walk and cycle instead of riding in a car. There was a war on, it had to be won, and that was up to all of us. Whatever had to be done, we did, and no grumbles. Soldiers, sailors, airmen and women were risking and losing their lives to defend us and keep us fed, some of whom were older men who would normally have retired or slowed down and were now working double shifts or two jobs. Who were we to complain? It was a challenge to which I responded with all I had, and found joy in it.

My aim was to eventually join the army; that was my goal. At school, Army Officers came to lecture us on the skills of army life and the strategies of war, and Navy Officers came to tell us of their experiences and battles; they inspired us and made us long to be part of this exciting stuff. What would we do when we left school? It was a choice of the Army, Navy or Air Force. Simple as that. On my seventeenth birthday, I walked to the recruiting office downtown from school, and registered for national service, as was required of all of us. The future opened a little more for me.

* * *

At a time that was about the middle of the war, I moved from day school to a boarding school in a seaside town about fifteen miles from home. Not the most ideal place for a school to be in such proximity to war activities, but where else? Along the sea promenade, now out of bounds to all, were placed guns of all types from machine guns to multiple pompoms. These were manned by bored soldiers who longed to have a go at something. A little plane towing a target far behind it flew along the shore line over the sea now and again for their practice, and they became so good at it that the target was shot to pieces before it was half away along.

Then one day came the real thing. It was a dull day with low cloud hanging over the town. Out of the cloud cover to the west of the town, two enemy aircraft suddenly dived and raced low across the town, machine gunning along the main roads and past our school as they went. They dropped two bombs near the railway station and the gas works, before disappearing back into the clouds. Everyone dove for cover and the racket was ear-splitting as every gun along the sea front opened fire, delighted to be able at last to have a go at "Gerry". It was over more quickly than it has taken time to write about it. The pilots must have thought it was great fun as they got away unscathed and flew home for lunch.

Through that summer of the last year of the war, tremendous things were happening around us: a gathering of strength and military forces, and a sense of power and purpose that filled us with excitement. The town and surrounding countryside were crowded with soldiers and their equipment. The side roads around our school were lined with parked lorries, armoured cars and tanks. These streets became temporary workshops and parade grounds. Every morning, the soldiers turned out to do a prescribed run as a keep-fit requirement, and we would join them before school. Everyone was waiting for the great day.

Twice I caught a glimpse of the famous General Montgomery, "Monty" to everyone. One day, as we walked along the road between our school buildings, two army motor cycles roared around the bend, closely followed by an army jeep. Sitting erect by the driver was the perky and confident Monty, going about his business, followed by two more motor cyclists. There was not even time to cheer. The second instance was on another day as we were on our way to the sports field, when we saw soldiers all running in one direction. What was up?

"Monty's on the Green!"

We joined them, sports forgotten, running for all our worth to see the great man on whom all our hopes were pinned. At the edge of the Green, we were brought up short by military police. Only those in uniform were allowed through. There he was, standing erect on top of a vehicle, black Tank Corp beret and ordinary battle dress uniform complete, surrounded by hundreds of enthusiastic soldiers who crowded in to listen to him as he poured out his confident message of encouragement and enthusiasm to them all. This was the man who was going to lead them into the great adventure and dangerous mission of finishing off the war. We, the bystanders, caught snippets of his speech as his clear, high pitched voice carried across the Green.

It was during this period that the great thousand-bomber raids took place over Germany in an attempt to destroy their war machine. On clear summer evenings, as far as one could see in either direction, to the East or West, inland or over the Channel, the skies were filled with four-engine Lancaster bombers with their even engine note and in open formation, steadily and purposefully making their way out across the sea to carry out their missions.

One Sunday evening, as we gathered for the evening Chapel Service, there was suddenly a different sound, drowning out the rest. It was the roar of a low flying bomber, little more than roof-top height, racing across the town. It just missed the Odeon Cinema, the highest building in its path which would have been crowded at that time, and crashed into the sea with an explosion that shook the town, and the blast from which broke most of the windows of the buildings along the sea front. Then, the incredible silence which always seemed to follow an explosion like that. We were silent too. What had happened?

The next day we read in the newspaper that one of the Lancaster bombers had suffered engine trouble following take-off. The Captain had ordered his crew to bale out over land, which they did safely. He had remained in the aircraft to keep it in the air, which he managed to do until it was over the sea. The story was given just four or five lines, stating the bare facts among the other news of the day.

I often think of that man, unnamed, an unsung hero of the highest order. Was he a youngster in his early twenties as so many of them were, or a married man with a family? We did not know. He was just another man doing his duty, fulfilling his responsibilities, fighting with the controls of the plane to keep it in the air, knowing he was going to die in a matter of minutes. Had he bailed out too, as he could have done, and it had crashed on the town with its full load of bombs on board, hundreds of people could have been killed, us among them. His was one more life lost among so many who died for their King and Country.

* * *

One morning, we woke to a great silence. We were puzzled, and looking from our dormitory windows saw the streets were empty. They had gone quietly in the night, every last soldier, lorry, tank and armoured car. It was D-Day.

What excitement as we followed the news of the final battle. School lessons were secondary; the news of the day came first. The back-up for the battle, as lorry convoys of supplies moved towards the sea ports, took the place of fighting men and their equipment around us. We were now well behind the action, and had to rely on the media for news. At the air base near us, one transport plane landed and another took off every five minutes, day and night. They flew in carrying first wounded men, then German prisoners, and flew back out loaded with supplies. The fighter squadrons moved away too, to back up the ground troops from bases nearer the action.

Eventually, as the fighting moved into Germany itself, we saw lorry-loads of men who had been freed from Prisoner of War camps, cheering and waving, driving up the main road alongside our village to in-land reception centres, after being flown in by the faithful and reliable Viscount transport aircraft. Some of these men had been prisoners for four years and more, and were obviously enjoying the first glimpse of their home country at last.

And then, to the absolute horror of the whole world, came the first-hand news relayed in the newspapers and over the radio news broadcasts of the terrible concentration camps, exposing to the free world the true character and warped minds of the Nazi regime that had enveloped and drawn into its evil doctrine a whole nation of normally sane people.

Conditions and shortages were increasingly evident as we moved into that last year of war. Europe was starving so our armies found, its infrastructure destroyed, and millions of people had to be fed and cared for as much as ourselves. Rationing of most daily requirements became even more severe. As farmers and farm workers, we were now recognised as important as fighting men, as the need for food became desperate. To our delight, we were allowed a double ration of bread and cheese, nourishing stuff for those doing heavy manual work.

I am proud to say that the farmers responded and produced the goods needed. In fact, we were told later that the farmers of Britain were the first industry to achieve their Government-set, post-war production targets. During the harvest time we often worked till ten o'clock at night, only stopping when the dew began to fall and the corn and cut sheaves were too wet to cut or stack, to knock off and head for home, supper and bed. And Mum always had a meal ready for us when we came in.

I was doing a full man's work by then; six feet four inches tall, I was stronger than most and, I must admit, a bit proud of the fact. But at least I felt that, although I was not a fighting man with all the dangers and glory that went with that, I was doing my bit for a country that had given me my birth and heritage.

When the end finally came, we were working in the fields. Word came somehow that the German armies had surrendered. This had to be celebrated! As soon as I could, I left the job I was doing and, with my friend Ian, ran across the fields to the railway station and boarded a train for Brighton. It was jam-packed with people, mostly cheering men and women in uniform. We joined them. A controlled indiscipline seemed the order of the day. Soldiers were wearing Women's Airforce (WAAF) caps, while the women wore soldiers' caps. Everybody was everybody else's friend. Kisses and hugs were exchanged at random, as we poured out onto the platform at our destination, into the streets and along the sea front.

The long-silent bells pealed out, lights previously darkened and hidden now blazed. We cheered, we sang, we laughed and hugged. We had won the war, as we always thought we would somehow, the alternative being unthinkable. Now it was here; this was VE Day, and we were going to enjoy and celebrate it. All a bit childish, I suppose, but the restrictions and shortages and disciplines of the past five years were discarded with joy, thrown overboard, because we were still alive and kicking.

All that had to be done now was sort the Japs out. Little did we realise in our euphoria that there were still men and women and whole countries under the vicious control of the Japanese army, and that the most violent fighting was going on, far away, to deliver them. In addition, the Communist regimes were trying to bring under their control and bondage those countries only just freed from Nazi control. A boy, two years my junior at school, won the Military Cross fighting them while I was still on the farm, working under the control of the authorities in Essential Services. I was just one of eighty thousand men in my category awaiting their call-up orders to become soldiers and go to relieve the men who had had five years of service overseas and wanted to come home. As I have mentioned previously, this call-up was postponed every three months for another three months, and was unsettling for me to say the least.

Although restrictions in many ways were gone, shortages remained of many commodities from petrol to potatoes. But the motivation of winning the war and doing all we had to achieve this was gone, to be replaced by the uninspiring job of winning the peace. Our hero, with his cigar, two finger V sign and rousing speeches, who had inspired and led us to victory, had been replaced by a rather dull man who, with his idealistic supporters, aimed to impose on us an uninspiring, dull and over-organised regime. Even those who had voted them into power seemed shocked by what they had done in rejecting the very people who had brought them through the darkest hours. Or so it seemed to me.

As for me, my Dad was dead; the farms I loved no longer offered a future for me; my home was broken up, the family dispersed, my Mother trying to cope with widowhood and two young girls in a house in town, and my own future was insecure and uncertain. I still worked on the farms, first one and then the other, but just for work's sake, really.

The challenge was gone. I certainly did not want to go into the army and stand sentry over a defeated enemy. I wanted out, to venture afield to pastures new, where I could be myself and control my own destiny. What and where was that to be? I had no idea. But I think a Higher Power did. In fact, I know now, so many years later, when there are few folks who still remember those exciting days, that my future and destiny were quite secure in those capable and far-seeing Hands.

Little did I realise it at the time.

5

INITIATION

"I write to you, young men, because you are strong."

1 John 2:14

Arriving at Hillwood Farm, in Chief Ikelenge's area of the Mwinilunga District, Northern Rhodesia, was the beginning of the rest of my life in a very real sense. Here, as a young man of unknown reputation, character and ability, I was welcomed into and eventually embraced by a branch of a family of great standing, who were held in the highest respect by the people of the Lunda tribe among whom they lived.

The founders of this family, Dr Walter Fisher and Mrs Anna Fisher, who had passed away more than ten years before, were still remembered with the greatest affection by the distinctive Lunda tribe. They had settled in the district forty years previously, and had brought and taught the Gospel of Jesus Christ widely amongst them. They had also brought medical and social help to these people and assisted them in moving towards improved standards of living and outlook.

The Doctor and his wife had raised their family here, each of whom in their years carried on the work and life ethics of their parents in greater or lesser ways. Among them was their son ffolliott, and his wife, Ethelwyn. Mr and Mrs ffolliott Fisher, and their children, were now doing their part at Hillwood.

Although maintaining an English way of life in many senses, and well aware of their roots, the Fishers were at the same time well integrated into local life and culture. Most were fluent in the Lunda language and communicated freely and easily with all those around them. Hillwood Farm, land granted to Mr F. in 1921 as an ex-war time army Officer, had become the home of this branch of the family, as well as a business centre bringing commercial activity to the area and employment for scores of people. The knock-on effect of this brought a degree of prosperity to this remote corner of their vast country, such as had not been known before.

I was introduced to a part of the ffolliott Fisher family that first afternoon by Mr F. whom I now knew, of course. Mrs Fisher, a powerful character of great ability and determination, presided over her home and surroundings with ease and authority. I next met Joyce, the eldest daughter, small, dark and efficient, and Anne, a taller, blond laughing girl of about eighteen with fair complexion and an easy manner who was to become a major factor in my life. In the background was a small girl of about twelve who was very shy and quietly flitted from room to room with suppressed giggles. The rest of the family were away at school or university, and one of the daughters was married.

I think my first impressions of this home and family were of a combination of ease and order. Dinner, my first meal with them, was a full and formal meal for which everyone prepared and assembled, bathed and dressed in what is now known as casual-smart attire. During dinner, we were waited on by a dig-nified "table boy", a mature man who knew his job thoroughly.

This meal was followed by coffee in the sitting room, where I was introduced to quinine, the prescribed antidote for malaria, and the family's unique home-grown and home-brewed coffee, served in tiny cups. Two Great Danes, enormous dogs who had been fed during dinner, plus a grouchy Alsation-Ridgeback cross, now came in with the remains of their food on their noses, which they tried to wipe off by nuzzling along the girls' house coats, and who swept the coffee cups off the low tables with their tails. A relaxed evening followed. There was much chatter, some cautious questions asked of me, and the BBC News crackling out over a large radio.

Then bed. I was given a small room facing out onto the grass quad which formed the centre of the house. After I was shown how to cope with a mosquito net, the house settled down for the night. This was my first experience of the quiet of an African night, with only the occasional animal, insect or bird calls to break the silence.

I did not have a specific job, title, or position in this establishment; nothing had been formally stated. Hence the next day, my first full day, I was a little concerned about where I really fitted in. It was a bit bewildering. I was asked to help Mr D., Mr Fisher's dour Scottish assistant who was known as "Wadizemba", the bender of iron. While working in the forge that morning, not my scene really, I was fascinated by the behaviour of the people around me. There seemed to be a stream of folk passing by the forge, and each person was greeted with great courtesy with a pause in the work for ceremonial handshakes. So completely different from the Sussex workmen I had known who, without a pause in what they were doing, would only manage a gruff "G'moornin".

Gradually I moved on and out into the wider aspects of this multi-activity set-up. Mr Fisher told me that I was welcome to live with them until things became clearer as to my future. He would pay me pocket money at a rate of £5 a month, and we would see how things went.

I was introduced to the cattle work and their comings and goings, the dairy work, and how to help in the selling store from time to time. What I did discover was that the more I involved myself in things the more I was given to do, even responsibility for overseeing certain jobs. I was taught to make butter by Joyce and that became my permanent early morning job. This was followed by seeing to the small animals, like pigs being fed and their sties cleaned out, then cycling out with Mr F. for the daily inspection of a gang of labourers making a new entrance road, which is still in use today.

There always seemed to be building going on of workers' houses and so on, and I learned to lay bricks, great heavy sun-dried things made of clay and soil, six inches by nine inches by twelve. I also learned how to thatch in the local way. I quickly discovered that whereas the local workmen had some shortcomings they also had incredible skills, especially with their homemade tools. The little axe was one: a blade made of old car springs, heated in a forge using a charcoal fire and ingenious bellows made of buck skin, and beaten into shape on a stone. Once the blade was red hot, it was fitted into a carefully shaped wooden handle cut from a tree. It was an incredibly efficient little tool. There was also the hoe for digging, which was far more effective than a spade or shovel. I was determined to learn how to use these tools properly, and I did learn much from watching and working with these men.

At the same time, I learned a bit of the language. There was constant chatter among them, a great deal of laughter, a lot of teasing and ribbing, and occasionally some growling. Task work was one way of getting the work done quickly and I learned to allocate such tasks to individuals or pairs of men working together, who would then proceed with their particular task and knock off work when it was done. Some of the men were more efficient and stronger than others, and I learned how to recognise that; others were expert at skimping jobs, and I learned how to detect that. That first year was one long learning curve, which I enjoyed greatly.

While there were servants in the house and garden to do the routine work from cooking to washing, cutting fire wood and weeding the flower beds, it did not mean that the family members lived in luxurious ease. Far from it. They all had their duties too. Joyce and Anne worked with the hundred plus orphans, from new-born babies to teenagers, all of whom lived and were cared for on the farm. Mrs F. had her gardens—veggies, fruit and flowers—and the household to oversee, besides the Orphanage and a home-run clinic to which people came from the villages all around as well as the farm-workers and their families. Any ailment could surface here, from the common cold to axe wounds in the head following a drunken fight. Mrs F. dealt with it all, aided by a stout lady called Nyachinyama. She had an incredible ability in diagnosing ailments, as well as in sorting out the skivers and work dodgers, or those who just came for a social outing. For the really ill or wounded, nothing was too much trouble. Hesitation in making necessary decisions was not in her lexicon, and her daughters followed hard in her footsteps.

I was encouraged to learn the language. The potential limitation in my usefulness, and for others too in this working environment, was lack of the ability to communicate. I tried hard to overcome this, but have never in all my life become fluent in the Lunda language, to my shame. A working knowledge I did acquire, and it got me by. But I can see now that I have lost a lot by not being able to converse widely with a group of people whom I came to admire and respect.

In some areas, I was able to give them leadership and set an example. I had been brought up to work physically; I was strong and fit, and I had learned from my Father that when there was a job to do, you did it. I learned leadership as time went on, but I also learned that if I was to command the respect of these discerning people it had to be earned. This was a challenge.

More and more, the cattle occupied my time. The herd comprised about fifteen hundred head. They were not all kept on the farm as some herds or groups of forty or fifty cattle were kept in camps far away in Chiefs' areas, usually two herds to a camp cared for by trusted herdsmen. At night, they were kraaled or penned in lion-proof pens made of poles, about four to five meters long, set upright in a trench half a meter deep and the soil tramped down. The poles were bound together with long lathes and tied tightly with bark rope stripped from trees.

Some herds, mostly cows and calves, were penned on the farm in large, covered sheds. Their calves were shut away at night in side pens, and the cows milked in the early morning. To achieve this, the cow's hind legs were tightly bound together with rheim, a rope made out of dried and treated cow skin. The calf was then brought alongside to suckle, and once the milk began to flow it was chased off and the milker then milked like mad until the cow would not let any more down. Effective, but to me a bit primitive.

What astonished me was that in the early morning, cold and wet sometimes, the milkers would turn out in the skimpiest of loin cloths but otherwise naked and shivering. They did their milking job puddling around in the half dark, their bare feet in the dung that had accumulated in kraals overnight. And then, as the sun rose warmly for another hot day, they would wash themselves down using hot water from a half drum heated over an open fire and put on a full set of clothes—hat, coat, the lot—and take the herds of cows out to graze in the bush all day, even if it was hot. This meant they did not soil their clothes and earn the fury of their wives who would have to wash them. Logical, I suppose.

It was hardly hygienic milk production, but it served well in the circumstances until a Jersey herd was introduced to the farm some years later. The milk production varied. Most of the cows calved towards the rainy season, so there was a flush of milk then. This all went to the dairy; milk for direct consumption was boiled, the rest separated for cream and butter or used for cheese making, and the skim milk fed to the pigs along with sweet potatoes bought from the villagers. Everything slotted together.

The nearest veterinary help was four hundred miles away, way beyond being any real or regular help. I spent a lot of time searching through veterinary books, trying to learn of the local diseases, their causes and cures. I became experienced in dealing with difficult births through sheer practice, never became very good at post-mortems, and I learned a lot of stockmanship the hard way.

Ticks were the problem, as they not only carried disease, but a surfeit of these blood-sucking pests caused debilitation.

About that time imported bulls, quarantined at the Government Research Station in the Southern Province, had brought with them a type of tick carrying a disease called Senkobo Skin Disease. A horrible thing, it spread like wildfire through the whole herd. The skin of infected animals developed hard crusts which spread all over the body and eventually down the legs, and the result was death.

An outside camp, about five miles away from the homestead near the Belgian Congo Border and alongside the great Kamata open plain, was turned into an isolation camp. At one time, we had nearly four hundred animals there. Weekly, I would go there with a team of men, cycling out and wading through the two rivers—the Sakeji and the Zambezi—to check and treat these suffering animals. We doused their bodies with oil from castor beans that grew wild in this area especially over the border in Angola. Mr F. had set up a purchasing department, and the village women brought this sticky stuff in by the gallon. Poured on and rubbed in, it softened the crusty skin, relieved the discomfort, and gave the suffering animals a chance to overcome and survive. The measure of success was limited, but we just had to do what we could. It was hard work handling these cattle, docile enough normally, but upset and unused to being herded up and secured in a narrow crush passage for treatment.

A year or two into my time at Hillwood Mr F., on advice from the distant Government Veterinary Department, built a cattle dip. This great concrete tank, narrow and long, was built into the ground and when full contained about 1,500 to 2,000 litres of dip-wash, a diluted chemical which at the start was an arsenic combination, jolly dangerous. The cattle had to plunge in at the deep end and swim through, getting a thorough soaking in the process. This effectively killed off any ticks.

Now the fun started. Strong collecting pens had been built, narrowing down to a passage or crush leading to a jump-off point at the deep end of the plunge dip, two meters deep. Into this the cattle had to jump, there was no turning back. The first time was no problem, they were new to this but the process had to be repeated weekly to kill new tick infestations, and these wily beasts remembered. Getting them into the crush was one thing—just about every animal had to be pushed in—but at the jump-off point they firmly braced their front legs to resist making the final plunge, and strong-armed heave-ho was required. The stress and excitement affected their stomachs and there was a ready and steady stream of loose dung (I can describe it in no other way than the "s" word) which was freely projected over anyone fool enough to get into the line of fire.

Few of the herdsmen were big or strong enough to provide the final push. So you-know-who, together with a few hands-on helpers, was constantly in that firing line as animal after animal was shoved into the tank. The noise was terrific; bellowing cows separated from their calves, and the helpers in the rear making their contribution by shouting and whistling as they chivvied the cattle towards the dip. The front-line boys—rear-end boys in effect, including myself—had the full benefit of the cows' stress and excitement. I was soaked in what we called back in England "FYM", or farm-yard manure; my clothes heavy with it. I was wearing my School First Fifteen rugby jersey, and although it had seen some stress and muddy moments in its normal life, it had never been subject to this treatment before. During the tea break and while waiting for the next herd I dashed to the house and jumped in a bath, clothes and all, after which, in a clean outfit, I returned to the fray. I think I must have bathed at least three times during that day. But we won in the end.

In fact, we won in more ways than one. The cattle settled down and became used to jumping into and swimming through the dip, making it a much quieter and less stressful operation. Even the calves managed, without ever having to be taught to swim. It was a weekly job as a tick's life cycle is five days, and they had to be controlled. This was achieved, and visible ticks became a thing of the past. Unexplained deaths decreased dramatically, and the Senkobo Skin Disease was brought under control and eliminated, an achievement of which I was both proud and encouraged to have been a part. There will always be problems but they can be overcome if recognised and realistically faced. Another lesson learned.

Another memory I have of those happy days was that I found an old grass mower, a horse-drawn type of what was called a reciprocating mower. This was an antique version of what I had known back home, the modern version of which I had used behind a tractor. Here I was on familiar ground. How it ever got there I have no idea, but it was on the scrap heap as no one knew how it worked. I now came into my own. Bits were missing but the essentials were there, and I made up the missing parts from scrap and wood. Eventually, I got the thing going. Drawn by two old oxen who were galvanised into sufficient speed by the racket going on behind them, we leapt into action to the cheers of the onlookers. I hopped onto the rickety seat and away we went, dodging around through long grass and actually leaving a swathe of mown grass behind us.

I don't know that we served much purpose as there were no nice, level meadows to mow. Grass cutting during the rains was a necessity in order to prevent wild fires developing around the thatched buildings in the dry weather. We did contribute to this a little, but the acclaim which was accorded to me in all this was quite out of proportion to what was actually accomplished. It was not long before the ancient machine was put back in retirement, this time with honour, and the grass cutting was done once more by workers swinging a universal African tool, the *chikwakwa*, just a bent piece of hoop iron, which nearly seventy years later is still regularly and widely used.

I have said that these were happy days. It was my very good fortune to achieve the love and acceptance of the Fisher family within their ranks. What meant even more to me was the confidence of Mr F. who, I realised, was giving me more and more responsibility and allowing me increasing room to develop. I sincerely hoped that I was also gaining the friendship and respect of the local Lunda people, many of whom I worked with daily, even though I massacred their language, and more often than not overstepped their cultural norms and taboos. They laughed at me, corrected me, guided me, and, on occasions, shielded me. I owed all of these good people a huge debt for my happiness. And I think it was all a healing process for me from the traumas of past years, as I carved a place for myself in this new and unfamiliar environment.

6

THE SOCIAL SIDE

"A merry heart maketh a cheerful countenance."

Proverbs 15:13

One of my Mother's sayings was that "All work and no play made Jack a dull boy". True, and although I had been raised on a very strict work ethic, I did appreciate the other side of this new life that I was now experiencing. I was never a keen or apt sportsman, yet I enjoyed a bit of fun and games, and was very interested in people—just as people. There was plenty of scope for all that in my new environment.

The family days were divided neatly into separate parts with meals as the fixed points. First, early morning tea, which was brought around to each bedroom by a puffing youth called Yoba, who in nervous tension pushed out his lips and blew through them like a surfacing hippo as he crept into each bedroom with a previously prepared tray.

Then up and to work: two to three hours of specific activity as each family member went about their various jobs. General work started at seven o'clock when Mr F. went into his farm office, outside which scores of workers had gathered. For ten minutes or so, together with Mr D. and myself, he got down on his knees and prayed for God's guidance and blessing on the day's work. Then he took roll call, which comprised an astonishing variety of names, and allocated the day's tasks. Cattle workers did not attend as they were already busy, but the two cattle foremen reported on their behalf. Then it was following up on individual jobs, dairy duties, dealing with minor crises, and making sure everything was running smoothly.

Breakfast was at nine: a substantial meal of fruit, millet porridge with milk and cream, bacon and eggs, toast and coffee, the latter dispensed from an ancient percolating pot with an empty marmite jar balanced upside-down on top as the original bit had been lost. Then prayers, an occasion and practice which seemed to bind the family together. These took place on the front steps of the house, where all the family plus any visitors, sat on the cold stone. Mr F. read from the Bible and then prayed, a wider prayer this time remembering the extended family members, their needs and doings, and things beyond. There are many photographs as witness to this central point in the day on the veranda steps.

It was then back to work, further afield this time for me, to wherever there was a need. Mr F. went to his office and banged away on a long-suffering typewriter. This was the only means of communication with the outside world in those days, apart from telegrams that in emergencies were sent from the nearest Post Office fifty miles away. All his business was conducted by this means: orders for store goods from London, or details of things like beeswax being dispatched for sale on the London market and addressed to his broker there.

For London business the Congo railways over the Border were used. Outgoing produce and incoming goods travelled by ship and rail and were loaded and off-loaded at the out-back railway station of Mutshatsha. The goods were carried between the farm and station on a contraption called a Push-Push—a very descriptive name for a vehicle of sorts that was propelled back and forth by five men along the dusty, winding fifty-mile connecting road through the bush. A unique and low-cost transport system, it was one that worked well but which required patience and careful input. One of the hazards until a wooden bridge was built was a small pontoon over the Muckleweji River that would capsize if not loaded with care to maintain balance.

Lunch was at one o'clock, either a cold meal of meat and salad, or another roast beef-and-veg affair. Then Rest Hour, a hallowed time when everyone retired to lie on their beds, read, sleep, and rest. Unheard of in my previous existence where it was back to work at two o'clock, here it was regarded as essential to maintaining good health and stamina in this sub-tropical climate. A jolly good idea too, especially as I was a keen reader and there was a plentiful supply of good books to choose from.

From three to four o'clock, there was a dash around to ensure the day's work and tasks were completed, to count the takings from the stores, and to see to any requests from workers. At four o'clock came tea, which was just that, with little cakes or scones, on the large veranda.

Work was now largely finished for the day, and there was time to do our own thing. We often played tennis. The court was a good one, surfaced with neat cow dung that was spread on and smoothed by hand by local women who did an excellent job. When dried, it gave a good surface, although not quite up to Wimbledon standards. The alternative to this past-time was a walk with the dogs who knew that it was their time and did not let anyone else forget.

As the sun set, I usually went to see the cattle coming home after their day's grazing in the bush, quietly crossing the river and making their way to their respective night kraals. The girls saw to any late needs with the orphan children, and Mrs F. would take a leisurely walk through her veggie gardens. Then it was bath, change, dinner, coffee and quinine, a restful evening, and bed. An ordered and satisfying day.

Retiring for the night, one felt a sense of completion and achievement in this productive environment. And it was produc-tive. Not only did it provide for the needs of the family (a secure and loving home) and all those other needs such as education and medical, and the occasional family holiday even as far away as Cape Town, but it went much further than that. Food provisions were supplied to the Mission Hospital and School thirteen miles away, to the School for missionaries' children just across the river, and to other expatriates living in the district, some receiving supplies daily and some weekly, conveyed mostly by carriers bearing great, long, baskets, who walked the distances there and back as a normal routine. Some less perishable stuff went much further, up to one hundred miles by the same means. Food and milk for the orphanage, milk for TB patients in the villages (gratis), meat once a week to order; there was a constant stream of orders for supplies to be sent out. Missionaries, Government Officials and passers-by also called in for fuel and a variety of goods from the shop, or "store" as it was called.

The farm and trading business was the central hub of the area. The trading department was not only selling imported goods, but was engaged in buying locally produced goods brought in from the villages far and near, even from Angola and Congo. Some items like dried fish was re-sold locally, and some was exported. Mr F. had perfected a process for purifying beeswax of which there was a plentiful supply, and this was sold for cosmetics on the London market. Honey in considerable quantities was also bought, refined, stored in great milk churns, and sold to Pharmacists on the Copperbelt in Central Zambia.

All this was not only a matter of economics. There was a social side to it too, of constant interaction between the individuals involved, as well as supporting and boosting the communal and service side of the area. I came to know many people from far and near, learning what they were doing and how they were doing it, what contributions they were making to the whole, how they fitted into the overall structure of life in this rapidly developing country, and how it all worked.

Missionaries there were in plenty, astonishingly so. Bringing their children to and from the nearby school was a four-times-a-year event; they travelled by car or truck, sometimes for two days, along dusty or muddy tracks through the bush from remote home stations and they then took the opportunity to stock up on necessities before returning home.

They all had personalities, and interestingly these came into clear and defined focus in this remote community. Some of them I came to admire greatly, people who could have made it big in their home countries but who were humbly giving their all to serve their God and the people. Others were living in what would have been considered elsewhere great poverty, but content to be as they were in fulfilling their calling and mission.

There were some serving and supporting those who served, and not a few even risking their lives as they went about their business. I remember one little, old lady who was a terrible driver, nevertheless she would drive through the night in the wettest and muddiest road conditions, sliding up and down steep hills, to take very sick patients to the hospital. Another was a nurse who spent her time combing through the villages to identify prematurely pregnant young girls in order to check them and get them to hospital where they could be given the help needed when the time came. Scores of these child brides had been dying previously, and she saved many lives.

Many of these folks paid the price in different ways, and there were times of health and mental breakdowns among them, and even neglected family needs, as they gave their all. Some did it with strength and joy; others I wondered why and how they had come as they struggled to make a contribution. They were certainly neither fitted nor able to cope. The culmination of this last group was, for me, when an American lady, a delightful, gentle but delicate person, died in childbirth for want of the correct blood type for a needed transfusion, leaving three little boys and a husband. Who had vetted these people, and who was giving them the support so evidently needed when they moved out of the care and security of their home environment?

There were others about whom I wondered, for different reasons. Their temperament, their weaknesses, their characters and their phobias came into sharp focus in these confined and challenging circumstances, showing their inability to cope or perform under pressure. I saw there was a great deal of difference between being a missionary on home-leave as I had previously seen them in England, and one coping with things in a very different scenario. Not the least challenge was having to get on with everyone around them, from whom there was no escape.

Having said that, there were many real characters who surfaced around us, who were a source of inspiration. One of these was the local Government District Commissioner, an Oxford Blue with a string of degrees. When I first saw him, he was wearing boots and shorts, was soaking wet and covered with mud. He was driving an overloaded Dodge Truck over the most terrible roads in the heaviest time of the rainy season, trying to get food to people who were cut off by swollen rivers and washed away bridges. A long way from his Oxford College, this was the type of man who administered the much-criticised Colonial Empire.

Another such character was a Portuguese settler from just over the border in Angola. He lived among the villages, married a local woman and had a large family of children; he sent all his sons to Portugal for education, and most probably and cheerfully broke every rule in the book. He was educated and widely read, spoke fluent but broken-sounding English, and entertained us with incredible stories when he visited Hillwood by illegally crossing the border.

Then there was Mr Raffy Raftopoulis, from the railway town over the border in the Congo. He owned and personally ran a huge trading store, stocked with everything imaginable. He could most days be found sitting at his table just inside the entrance door, talking loudly—rather shouting—in a bewildering variety of languages from French to Swahili and various tribal languages. Simultaneously, he kept a sharp eye on everyone and what they were doing, from the latest visitor to his many salesmen.

To say Raffy was a character would be an understatement. He was what one could only call a good-hearted rascal, who could be the essence of reliability and honesty while bending or breaking every rule that stood in his way. It was a tonic to visit him, although a danger to drink his ultra-strong coffee. He begged me to leave "Mr Feeshair" and come and work with him. He promised he would show me how to really make money, and probably would have shown me a great deal else besides, the like of which would have sent my resilient mother into a dead faint. He fell in love with a German missionary lady and proposed to her, which scared the life out of her so badly that she ran for cover to her home country.

"I am mad about 'er," he confided in me one day.

He was a really good-hearted man, although not very inspiring at first sight in his carpet slippers, baggy trousers, massive belly, loose shirt with no collar, stubbly chin and huge bush hat. He acted as agent for Hillwood, seeing to the dispatch of outgoing goods sent from Hillwood and the off-loading of goods coming in by rail, all with care and accuracy. I never heard Mr F. complain of his services.

I must also mention another character, this time an Irishman. He was the Veterinary Livestock Officer stationed four hundred miles away who came to visit a few times. His conversation, his stories, his whole approach to life, were a source of constant entertainment and delight. I am not sure his visits were of much technical help with the cattle; coming from Northern Ireland, he did not know much more about local problems than I did. But after his visits, he left behind a wealth of amusement and laughter that kept us entertained for days. I still laugh at his stories today, when I remember them.

I have been speaking of the "imports", the expatriates of various varieties. But that leaves out the heart and soul of the community. There were so many of them. The local Chief, a gentleman by any standards, who patiently taught me many things. Handsome, smiling, at ease in any company, he attended our wedding (I'm getting ahead of myself) and made an amusing but kindly speech.

The head cattle man was called Kamungwamba. As a small boy, he had come up to the interior from the coast along with travelling ox wagons in earlier days, and had somehow been left behind when they returned. Now he was an authority figure and right-hand-man to the *Mwanta*, Mr F.

Chitesenge was another; a small, tough, but aged man, who had leprosy and had survived smallpox. He herded a large group of heifers for the farm in a remote camp, and could travel immense distances on foot with greatest ease.

Fulayi was a tall, strong man who ran everywhere. He was a terrible fighter but a great worker; fearless and loving a challenge, I worked with him and he for me for many years. My sort of man!

Nzewu was a real friend, a quiet man who was a very experienced hunter and a crack shot with a rifle. He taught me so much about the bush and could follow a trail at a fast walk that I could not see or even detect in any way. He had a great sense of humour and I never heard him boast. Our children loved him; they crowded around him when he came and sat in our kitchen, chattering away with him and showing him their picture books, which strangely he could only decipher when turned upside down. His son Daniel was our cook for years.

I cannot leave out Mazaza, the deaf and dumb man, a character of note who, with his pantomimed stories, facial expressions and physical actions, could bring everything and everybody to a hysterical, laughing halt. He would have made a fortune on the London stage. When he arrived on the place, all work came to a stop as he entertained the appreciative audience.

Kajomoto, the lorry driver, had been in the army and driven lorries all the way up to East Africa and in Burma during WW2, and had the most sarcastic turn of phrase when annoyed. I remember him bringing in a loaded lorry through pouring rain and over appalling roads, having mended a broken main leaf spring by cutting a supple piece of timber from the bush and binding it on with bark rope.

Makina, shaped like a prize fighter, was a gentle giant who had the most wonderful chuckle and an athlete's springy walk. Musanvu the gardener could imitate the parrot, also teaching it things he should not have; he served Mrs F. faithfully in all she demanded of him in her garden, and seemed to know her wishes before she made them known. And so many more. I was so fortunate to have known and worked with them all. This was the social and community side of our life in that remote but significant corner of the country.

The regular, daily routines were encroached on at times, especially at Christmas. I still remember my first, one of many at Hillwood. The family gathered, coming from school, university, and Peggy and Gordon with the first grandchild. There were guests as well. Mrs F. was in her element with the challenges of catering and accommodation over and above her usual routine.

Work schedules still went on but there was a lot of fun and additional activities. Not least was the Christmas Party to which mostly missionaries from the surrounding area came. The house was bursting. Some welcomed the opportunity to let their hair down, while others displayed previously undetected talents in playing the fool. Only the dour but lovely elderly Scottish nurse, to whom many owed their lives and health, left early in disapproval.

I thrived in this environment, and grew in confidence and vision. I had been told when younger, back in England, to work hard and play hard, but to never mix the two. Somehow, this was not true here; the two seemed to blend, and it was exhilarating. At this stage, I never yearned for home, never regretted the decision I had made almost on an impulse. A foundation was laid in my life in those years that was of lasting value.

* * *

Before I move on, I wish to highlight and bring into focus two people who were of great significance to me during those years. One was Mr F., Walter ffolliott Fisher, second son of the Doctor. He came into my life two and a half years after my father passed away. He was another unique man, steadfast and faithful, principled and focused. Born in Ireland, he was raised at first in his parents' remote home in the African bush. From there he progressed to school in Ireland, and briefly to university in Bristol until World War 1 started. Together with hundreds of thousands of other young men he volunteered for the army, was commissioned into the Sherwood Foresters as a second lieutenant, and hurled as a teenage Officer into the carnage in France.

Wounded three times, he came out of that experience seriously crippled and hardly able to walk. He was then 21 years of age. After long spells in hospital, he returned to Africa and his parents' home. He was very restricted in what he was able to do when he arrived but his father, an accomplished surgeon, undertook in those limited and primitive conditions a bone graft operation. This was a rare thing at that time under even the best of conditions but it restored his ability to walk, although he remained lame and used a walking stick for the rest of his life. Then, with his parents' help, he pulled the bits and pieces of his life together, and had to decide what to do with the rest of his years.

For a start, he married Mrs F. who was a teacher at the Mission School. He then applied for and was granted an ex-serviceman's allocation of land alongside the beautiful Sakeji river, thirteen miles away. With twenty or so head of cattle from his father, he started to farm and to trade, buying local produce for resale and importing consumer goods for sale to the local people. The primary objective was to supply the Missions with food and other needs. As he told me himself, he had little knowledge of farming, cattle, or business as he set out on this venture, or even the value of money. But he learned, and learned fast, and in the years ahead built a substantial cattle herd and a thriving business, becoming a respected and valued personality in the country. His support of individual missionaries and their mission, his input into their needs in every way, and the open home and caring welcome that he offered was more than significant. And all this he did in a quiet and matter-of-fact way, together with Mrs F. They were very much a team.

What sort of a man was he? For a start, he was a gentleman, in the real meaning of the word. His courteous manner, his ready smile, his friendliness, his humour always so near the surface, all contributed to his profile. He had a love for people, a simple and clear approach to right and wrong, and had the highest standards of uprightness. His complete lack of concern about his own disability and his almost casual determination to do what had to be done, was an inspiration to me and, I am sure, to many others. He had an authority with those he employed and a respect from the Lunda people as a whole, which they willingly gave, all based on their discerning assessment of him as a man to be trusted. What you saw was what was there, and it was wise never to underestimate him, as some did. He was easily hurt, because he saw things simply and did what he was convinced was right, uncompromisingly.

Physically he was not tall, his lameness affected that. But he was good looking, upright, with an open face and manner, and moved with confidence even when he was in pain, as he was in his later years. He never spoke of his ailments, and rarely of what must have been the horrific experiences of his war years. He had a very good eye, and would have been an excellent sportsman. He even played tennis doubles, with a deadly eye for the ball and a long reach that you underrated to your cost.

He read widely, a favourite pastime, and kept up with world affairs and doings. He was very British with a strong sense of loyalty and belonging. Every Christmas day, with reverence and even awe, the family would gather to hear the King's speech, and later the Queen's, in complete and unusual silence. As the National Anthem was played, Mr F. struggled from his low chair by the radio to stand erect, proud and strong, and with great respect.

He was a huge influence on my life, and I have always been grateful that events, difficult though they were for me at the time, had led me to come under his influence and guidance.

The other person I must write of before I move on was his fourth daughter, Anne. When I first met her, she was a tall, fair-haired, laughing teenager. Uncomplicated, easy-going and caring, she was very attractive, and appreciated and loved by all. My vision of her now, as she was then, is of a young woman surrounded by a group of teenage Lunda girls, all of whom seemed to be laughing and chatting freely. She was one of them, and they knew and loved her for it. She was adored by her boy cousins who often came to stay. I heard one of her sisters comment once: "All the boys love Anne, because she plays with them."

As time went by I could see that she was a little under the shadow of her university-going sisters, under-rating herself and I dare say being under-rated. Not that she was aware of it. Upon leaving school she worked with her Mother in the Orphanage, caring for children and babies, at which she was brilliant. She displayed an ability in medical things, especially diagnosis, with a simple, tender loving care that in later years sometimes even surprised doctors. On at least one occasion to my knowledge, she brought back to full health and strength a baby on whom the doctors had given up.

People trusted her instinctively, and have done all her life. She had compassion and quick understanding for all. She was fearless and strongly principled, and when called upon could deal with the most difficult and sensitive situations. When still in her twenties, she was able to lovingly and clearly explain to a bewildered elderly couple that their only son had committed suicide. She could well have been a nurse like her sister Joyce, or even a doctor given the chance, but for some strange reason that chance never came. She was classified as the least academic of them all, in spite of her string of distinctions in her school-leaving exams. She would just have to marry a farmer, they said and (thank God) she did. But that is another story. It was once whispered in my ear that I had got the pick of the bunch. I was inclined to agree, although I loved and respected them all.

I knew that it was Anne who was the girl for me. Convincing her was another matter. Added to that was the fact that I was up against three different cultures. In the one I had come from, a friendship moved into an easy courtship, and then an engagement. Simple. However, Anne's parents were still rather Victorian in their view of things. The man had to ask permission of the parents to even think of their daughter in terms of eventual marriage. I was severely told off for broaching the subject with Anne before going that route. And then there was the local African view within the Lunda culture. They were very uncomplicated, and simply decided that Mr F. had imported me to marry one of his daughters; which one was immaterial. These girls were of marriageable age, so what was the hold-up? With their usual perception they quickly worked out that it was to be Anne; "*tonda*" was the word they used, I had "*tonda'd*" her, which means "named" or "chosen".

From then on, we, or at least I, not only had to be careful but discreet as well, which young people in love rarely are. I fretted under this scrutiny and the fact that it was imperative in this family's culture that they must never put a foot wrong in the eyes of those amongst whom they lived. Until we were officially engaged we never went anywhere alone; that was taboo. I could never single Anne out for attention or in conversation during the daytime when there were people around. Had I not been discreet, which was not my nature, I knew I would be asked to pack my bags and move on elsewhere. I was not going to let that happen.

Our times together were limited to late evenings when the staff had gone home, and we had to make the best of that. My duty was to switch off the lighting power plant engine last thing, when all were in bed, but one evening I forgot as we were happily having a one-to-one chat-time sitting on a wall in the garden. We were brought to reality by someone calling out my name and asking if I had gone to sleep, and what about the engine? Far from it! Anne quickly disappeared into the darkness, while I mumbled "Sorry" and went to switch off the engine. But we survived, in fact our relationship blossomed, and eventually we became officially engaged, confirmed by a low-cost opal ring, fortunately Anne's favourite gem stone. It was all I could afford at that stage. I was thrilled; I had got my girl, and we were on our way.

Anne went on to become a wonderful and loyal wife, and a devoted and loving mother with the gift of communication that has held our family together through difficult times, and still does. She also has a discernment that is not always logical, she just knows, and she is so often annoyingly proved right.

To attempt to sum Anne up, she was and still is wonderfully loyal, compassionate and understanding. As the Book of Proverbs says, "A good wife who can find?" She was never a push-over though, and took a lot of convincing to start with. It is seventy years now since we began our life together, and we are still going strong.

7

LIONS, LORRIES AND THE LAW

One of the weekly routines at Hillwood was butchery day, every Thursday. This was always a day that created much interest and some excitement, as meat, or the lack of it, loomed very large in the food thinking of the local people. There was even a word for it in their language, "*Dikwilu*", which means "meat hunger". It sometimes seemed from remarks they made that they only felt they had really had a meal when meat was a part of it. Even very honest people could be led astray when the opportunity to get a bit of extra meat on the side presented itself. For this reason, hunters were highly respected, and also very sought-after husbands by girls and their parents.

At midday each Wednesday, an ox and usually an old cow as well, were selected and shot with a .22 rifle. A shot from as far away as ten yards placed squarely in the centre of the forehead was quite sufficient as a *coup de grâce* for anything but mature bulls who have a solid and impenetrable bone protection, common in all bovines. The carcasses were then skinned by willing hands, and the sides hung up in the butchery ready for butchering the next day. The "innards" were taken in a wheel barrow down to the river, washed clean and returned. All neat and tidy. But the pungent smell still hung in the air and was wafted around on the breeze, resulting in a disturbed night to follow.

Hyenas picked up the smell of blood from afar, and centred in on the cause of it with their hideous cries, more like a yodel. The house dogs who slept on sacks in the grass quad of the house, responded with gusto. Every time a hyena whooped they leapt to their feet and rushed for the narrow exit, barking hysterically and banging the door open as they all tried to go through it at once. This was repeated every hour or so and seemed to be accepted as routine by the family for Wednesday nights. I found it a bit disturbing to say the least.

One night while this was going on, one of the girls came to my bedroom door and quietly called: "Come and listen to the lions."

I joined the family on the veranda which faced out across the river and beyond, from where we could hear the hunting call and rasping grunts of two lions, far out on the plain, who had also picked up the scent. That was a first for me. Lions were not common to the area; in fact, there were only two other occasions when lions or news of them invaded us.

One such occasion was during my second Christmas there, when a lioness and her four half-grown cubs spooked some cattle at an outside camp and made a kill. They were followed up by Gordon, Peggy's husband, who was an experienced hunter. He came up on them as they slept off their feast in the shade of a tree. They leaped up when he whistled, and he shot three of them. I question now if this was necessary at all, as they were only passing through and would not have continued to be a threat to the cattle. The others made off rapidly; they were probably on a journey to somewhere as lions do travel long distances sometimes.

The other time was when an old lion tried to make a kill in a grazing herd during the day. He must also have been on his travels and could not believe his luck in coming across this opportunity.

However, although he made an attempt he only managed to scar one or two cattle, but failed to kill. He must have been past his prime. The stories told by the veteran herder of this incident were the most exciting part of this episode. Lions were not a serious threat in those days.

* * *

In the light of the present day and the universal awareness for the need of Wildlife and Ecological Conservation, as I look back on my first days in Africa and earlier, it is hard to comprehend how unaware were even the best of people of this urgent matter. In the very early days of the coming of Westerners into the interior of this vast continent, there was an abundance of wildlife and hunting for pleasure, profit, or even fame was quite an acceptable thing. This included Kings and Presidents from the West.

The truth is that the great hunters, so called, of those earliest days set the pace in this. Their activities and practice of shooting unremittingly was in fact destroying a heritage which was not theirs. The indigenous people did hunt, mainly with spears, bows and arrows, and traps, and were very skilled at it. But their hunting was part of a self-sustaining ecology to which they contributed as well as from which they reaped.

It was the coming of the powerful rifle with its telescopic sights and the organised expeditions that triggered the wholesale destruction of the plentiful wildlife. All in the name of sport. Anything that moved was in danger, and in reading stories of the so-called great hunters of those days, it is appalling to realize the wanton and mindless destruction.

Two famous hunters, high profile men from whom so many others took their cue in later years, are noteworthy. One shot every elephant he saw, big or small, and rhino as well, for their ivory and horns. These were loaded on to waiting wagons for transport to greedy markets, while carcasses were mostly left to rot. Without a qualm, he wrote books about it with full details. The other, also an author of his exploits, had an official Government contract in East Africa to shoot four hundred rhinos.

And there were more of the same. Their prized adventure stories contributed to a mind-set which is hard to imagine today, but in my early days it was still very real. Any animal was a target, from monkeys and leopards to elephant, and the skins and other trophies were traded with impunity. There were laws in place under the colonial administrations, but these were largely ignored, even if folk were aware of them.

Some weeks after I arrived, it was arranged for me to take Saturdays off work and go hunting. I had done a certain amount of rough shotgun shooting on farms in the U.K., but this was new to me. Led by a very skilled tracker and hunter called Nzewu (his hunting name after the black hunter ant) I set off into the bush on my first outing. By what I later realised was a complete fluke, and after a lot of walking through trackless bush, we came across a young sable bull. Taking a long shot I wounded it, and eventually killed it. To my shame. I realised later it was probably the last of its species in that area; I have never heard of another and I still regret having done this. At the time, I was acclaimed as having done a wonderful thing. A leg was sent to the Chief as a tribute, other gifts of meat were dispensed around, and I was congratulated all round.

For the next ten weeks, I went out every Saturday with Nzewu, intent on further building my reputation. No such luck. We walked for many miles through the bush and I learned quite a lot about bush craft, but saw nothing else that moved beyond a glimpse of a few roan antelope one day, who quickly took off when they caught our scent. The bush was bare and barren of any visible game animals. This cured me of so-called hunting in this context.

In all my years in this country, apart from the sable, I have only shot two oribi—beautiful little creatures—one puku ram, and one very angry young leopard by the light of the car because it was caught in a trap which I had not set. And that was too much. Unknowingly however, over the next ten years I overstepped the hunting laws and straight common sense in many ways, and was quite unaware I was doing it. It was the accepted thing. But several things changed my mind.

The first was meeting up with other men who had a concern for restricting hunting as it was known. They were Government appointed Honorary Game Rangers, and strangely enough I was elected at a meeting I attended to join with them in this work. One of them whispered to me when this happened,

"Watch out you don't have to arrest yourself!"

That was a wake-up call for me!

The second was seeing first-hand the effect that "hunting" had on otherwise rational and respected people. It was like a drug, and tended to dominate other vital things in their lives, such as their family and work.

As often as not, it also led to clashes with the authorities at worst, or just gave them bad reputations with those distant authorities who had their own ways of gathering information. Although, of course, the hunters were greatly appreciated by the local people who reaped the benefit of the meat without having to work for it. Additionally, there was the rapid decline of wild animals within their own habitats, increasingly noticeable as one travelled around. In saying all this, it is worth noting that sixty years ago there was a Government-paid bounty for killing wild dogs, five pounds each, and in one well known cattle-ranching area in the country, cheetah were classified as vermin to be shot on sight. It boggles the mind now, but for me it took a long time to sink in, as I guess it did for many others.

I emphasise the amazing change of mind-set in place now over wildlife conservation in this Twenty-First Century, which is evident in the enormous effort and expense poured into the preservation of endangered species. Strict hunting controls, anti-poaching methods, game parks and game-farming are some of the methods used today, as well as educational input on many levels.

At Hillwood today, although there is still a large herd of cattle, there are now extensive and well-fenced game areas where many species have been introduced or re-introduced and which are protected and managed by the current active members of the family. This, I may add, for the good of the local population who are benefiting from it in every way, and with the encouragement of the traditional Chiefs and Government authorities. Hunting does continue in this environment but is now very controlled and limited to animals of trophy value (usually old bulls of their species which have passed a natural "use-by" age) and effectively helps to finance the conservation work, which is very costly.

Endangered sub-species are also preserved in these vast enclosures, and even blood-typed for purity. A disease-free buffalo breeding herd of some hundreds is a part of this project, originally created by isolating calves at birth from their mothers in other herds elsewhere to prevent them from being infected with endemic disease carried by most of this species. The herd is held in this controlled environment and is a valuable and increasing breeding nucleus from which distribution can be made further afield. All this has happened within my time, and it is great to see this remarkable and enlightened development.

* * *

Significant changes in other areas have occurred throughout Central Africa, and perhaps the most significant is in communication. In my earliest years at Hillwood, it was the postal service from the nearest Post Office fifty miles from the farm that kept us in touch with the outside world. Mail was couriered by bicycle either way, once a week, to coincide with the weekly "Mail Bus" that only came that far. Joleki was the man for this job, our link with the outside world. A bit of an entrepreneur, he owned three bicycles, and youngsters from his extended family acted as the couriers. Urgent telegrams were also sent as one-offs by this means too, and it all worked efficiently and swiftly. A bit basic perhaps, but a great improvement on the earlier days when old Doctor Fisher had mail runners travelling on foot to Broken Hill, a mining town situated more than four hundred miles away, the site of the nearest Post Office and railway terminal. It was a three-month round trip for these men who blithely did it on foot along bush paths. One man was dispatched monthly to make sure there was a consistent and regular service. All a bit mind boggling in these days of cell phones and emails and other forms of instant communication.

Roads were also quite basic in those days although an advancement on the narrow, winding bush paths, worn bare by constant foot travel, which the early travellers had used. Long before my time in this area, travel had been an expedition for any family. Father went on foot or on a bicycle; mother in a hammock carried by two men; small children in box frames called "meat safes" covered by mosquito wire to keep biting flies off, also carried by two men. Anne remembers travelling this way as a small child, safe in her "box", with her pillow and teddy bear. Accompanying them would be any number of up to a hundred men carrying camping equipment, food and other luggage. Twenty-five miles a day by this means was good going.

By the time I came on the scene, cars had become a part of life for those who could afford them. Swathes had been cut through the bush by hand, soil built up to form a raised road surface, and drains dug for water to run off. These earth roads could be very wet and soggy, even collapsing in the months of heavy rain, but throwing up clouds of dust in the dry season. Their surfaces were in constant need of repair.

Bridges over the rivers were made of timber cut from the nearby forest, and held together by wooden pegs, cut and fashioned there on the spot. Works of art, they were usually built under the direction of an ancient local man who had learned the skill. However, they did get washed away in times of flood, which was a problem. The alternative over wider rivers was a locally-made pontoon, but these could also capsize if not balanced correctly.

Along these roads we travelled by car, in those days usually large American types such as Chevrolets and Fords. On long trips, it was wise to carry a shovel, an axe and a hoe in case of getting stuck or having to cut a fallen tree from the road. Also, a spare spring complete, or just a main leaf, as these could get broken. And of course, other smaller spares such as fuel filters, fan belts and universal joints.

Another essential was food and water. I have eaten many a breakfast by the roadside, cooked over a smoky fire: bacon, eggs, the lot, all washed down with tea made from smoky-tasting water. That was car travel.

In my early years, there was further progress. Mr F. bought a lorry, a six-ton Chevrolet, which was a huge advance for the farm and business. On the day it arrived, a man presented himself at the office to be the driver, coming unasked from a local village. Mr F. had not yet reached that point in his thinking, but in his humorous way just said,

"Well, you name it, we've got it, even in this remote place!"

Kajimoto had been a truck driver in the Northern Rhodesian Regiment during World War 2. He had driven along bush roads to East Africa and on to Abyssinia, and then in Burma. He wore a jaunty red Fez, and had a caustic way of expressing his displeasure to anyone who annoyed him.

He performed some amazing feats in bringing the goods home under the most appalling conditions. He once arrived at the farm after a long trip of some days to the Copperbelt, making his way along sodden roads in the heaviest rains, to bring in much needed supplies. The lorry brakes had failed and were non-functional, and a spring main leaf had broken, snapped right through under the weight of the load while crashing along uneven surfaces. He had managed the drive without brakes, no problem, up and down some pretty steep hills and crossing over streams. He had cut a strong piece of sapling from the bush, shaped it, jacked up the lorry and fitted it in place to replace the broken main spring blade, all bound together with strips of bark rope, also cut from the bush trees.

In time, buses also started to venture into this remote part of the country run by a company called Thatcher and Hobson. This bus-line was known locally as "Satcher", and carried mail, small loads of goods, and an overload of travellers, all packed in on seats and the floor. During the dry season there was little problem other than routine breakdowns causing delays, and choking dust. But in the rains, when the dirt roads collapsed or just deteriorated into slippery mud, these great vehicles ploughed through, leaping and rocking over the rocks and deep holes, or slipping and sliding, sometimes almost travelling sideways. When the driver saw that a stretch was impassable and they could become completely bogged down, he would stop, all the passengers would dismount and, under his direction, would cut poles in the bush and lay decking over which the bus could pass. All this was undertaken cheerfully and without complaint. The object was to get to the destination; time was not an issue and difficulties were there to be overcome.

It was a two-day journey for us to the nearest town of note where supplies could be obtained and loaded. In time, I was trusted with these buying trips. We would leave home before daylight on a Monday morning, carrying long lists of things to buy, together with lots of cash and open cheques. Once we reached town, there were three days of running from place to place, loading drums of fuel, buying spares, groceries and goods to sell in the farm stores. I became quite good at selecting the traditional "*chitenge*" cloth, of which there were many colours and patterns, which would please the local ladies back home and sell well. We bought most of our trading goods from the Indian wholesalers, of whom there was a wide choice and who were always efficient and helpful.

If all went well, we would reach home by Friday evening. This often meant driving at night to gain time, a tricky thing as after an hour or so I would begin to doze. This would pose the danger of running off the road and hitting a tree. So, the driver and I, Kajimoto's successor who had the same sleep problem as me, would change over every hour.

On two different occasions, I collected a load of young bulls from the railway in Ndola, and drove them up to the farm. Due to the threat of tsetse fly in some areas, we had to travel at night; during the day, we would park and light smoky fires up-wind from the lorry to drive off the tsetse flies and protect the bulls. Feeding and watering the bulls on the road was difficult, and we had to get through with the least delay. There were no casualties, I am pleased to say.

Eventually, tarred roads along with steel and concrete bridges came into being, and travel time we had counted in days we could now count in hours, eating pre-made sandwiches and drinking coffee out of thermos flasks along the way. But it had all been fun, and a challenge which I, for one, enjoyed.

These days, we are a lot more civilised and developed, but I am not sure we're that much more efficient. There are still difficulties to overcome, even though rather different. Mysterious things like permits and licences, controls and restrictions, have all taken the place of the old challenges that were clear and obvious and could be faced up to. The call for endurance in the contest of overcoming challenges has been replaced by the more passive need for patience and acceptance, which in my view is more frustrating. I rather liked the old days! And we certainly did have a lot of fun.

8

THE GOOD, THE BAD,
AND THE UGLY

"Think it not strange."

1 Peter 4:12

In one sense, I would like to have ended the story at this point, but that would not be honest, or give the full picture. Life includes the whole thing from beginning to end. Or at least as near the end as one can go.

The fact is that after two years and more at Hillwood Farm, I was getting restless. Several reasons contributed to this. One, it was my nature, certainly at that time. I had done all that I could there, or so I thought, and wanted to move on. It had also become obvious to me that although the family had welcomed and included me in their home life so warmly and beyond what one would normally expect, never-the-less this was a family set-up as far as succession and the future was concerned, and I did not see where I would fit into this. Nor, I think, did they.

I was also ambitious and impatient, perhaps beyond reason, and wanted to get on with my life. In short, I wanted to run before I had hardly learned to walk. At the back of my mind, I wanted a place of my own where I could put into effect what I had learned and felt I could do. And I wanted to get married. I wanted to be an established farmer in my own right, in my own home, with my own family around me.

Whatever the reasons, I felt I needed to move on. I had already made some tentative enquiries as to possibilities, and even been offered a job on one of the most progressive farms in the country owned by a man who had married Anne's older cousin. However, I was not altogether happy about that, so I backed off. The owner, part of the extended family, had quite rightly approached Mr F. first. Although he was quite willing to release me, I realised I was now beginning to be useful to him, and it would be wrong to leave at short notice. I was also not quite brave enough to take the plunge at that particular moment.

This is not the story of a romance or anything like it, but the truth was that the tall, blonde fourth daughter of the family, Anne, was my idea of the wife I wanted. So, without first approaching her father or mother (for which I later got my knuckles rapped), I went for it. I was determined not to lose this girl. Eventually she agreed and we were married. I was twenty-two; she was eighteen months younger. Perhaps our romance and the development of our relationship was not always smooth. It rarely is for two strong-minded young people. The point is that we were in love, which is not always easy to define but does help in surmounting most difficult situations. More importantly, our love for and appreciation of one another developed into a strength and standing that could and did help us overcome those unlooked-for difficulties that came our way.

Our wedding was pretty tame as far as weddings go these days, but it had its funny sides as well as being meaningful and real. We asked Anne's Uncle Wilfred to marry us, a lovely, quiet and gentle man who was a missionary. The wedding took place at Kalene Hill Mission, and is still recorded in the Marriage Register there, I'm sure. My mother and brother Norman came out from the U.K. to support me. Norman was my best man, but I think he was a bit out of his depth in this setting.

Invited people, family and friends, came from all around the country as well as from the Congo and Angola. Weddings seem to attract these folk as a bit of the unusual. They came to wish us well, too, and we appreciated that. Some brought tents, and camped around the garden at Hillwood. However, most of the congregation at the Church were local people who were not only well-wishers but who probably came for the show.

I waited for Anne, sitting in the front row of the Mission Church on a hard bench, with Norman beside me. Three of Anne's sisters sat behind us. Crisis. Where were the Order of Service hand-outs that had been carefully designed and printed in the far away town? A loud whispered conversation took place behind me. Where were they, where were they last seen? Sheila said she had seen them in Anne's room. Joyce's response to that was, "You wouldn't find an elephant in there this morning!" What should be done? Uncle Wilf rose to the occasion, and after Anne had arrived and we were standing at the front, he announced a hymn in Lunda which everyone knew and sung with gusto. I am not sure if it was appropriate for the occasion, but that did not seem to matter. It was a rousing start to the ceremony.

Apart from my standing on Anne's beautiful dress after we rose from kneeling for the blessing, and pinning her to the floor, ("Get off my dress, will you!"), all went well, and it was a lovely Ceremony. We stepped outside the thatched Church where a number of Anne's Lunda teenage girl friends from the Orphanage in their lovely colourful clothes and blouses, held branches of palm trees in an archway for us to pass under as a walk of honour. Many photos were taken, and then we departed in my new one-ton farm truck for Hillwood.

The Reception there was a happy affair; speeches were made, good wishes were showered on us, and we eventually departed to drive thirty miles to the family's holiday cottage near the lovely falls on the Luakera River. It had been a good day after which we enjoyed a few days by the river. The honeymoon being over, we departed for our new home on our own farm. The thatching on my "home-made" house was just finished in time, and we settled down to work out our lives together.

I wish I could say that we lived happily ever after, but few married couples can do that. However, neither of us have ever regretted it, or that we got married so young. Looking back, I can see that I was quite irresponsible in doing this as I was hardly established in life and had little to offer, other than my dreams and ill-founded ambitions. But we ploughed on through the normal rough and tumble of our early married life, and are as happy about it all now as we were then.

I will leave that part of my story just there.

* * *

During my last year working at Hillwood I had been looking at maps showing designated Crown Land areas that could be allocated for farm development. To recall again the profound statement made to me by my father's friend some years before:

"Russell, in stature you are more than a man . . ."

I was six feet four inches, so no argument there.

". . . in ability you are almost a man . . ."

I could do most things that came my way.

". . . but in experience you are still far from being a man."

At the time he said it, I was suitably reduced to size by the last bit as he was right. Now, at that stage of my life it was still true, but there was really no-one to put the brakes on. I forged ahead, looking carefully on the map and on the ground at some undeveloped areas available for allocation. I wanted to start from scratch. I eventually selected an area near the mining town of Chingola, about three thousand acres in size, which was regarded by Government Land Allocation Authorities at that time as suitable for a medium size farm. I made my application, and was granted a long lease.

In early 1950, I left Hillwood. Driving the one-ton truck that I had bought, on which was loaded my kit and the ten men I had recruited, I set out on my own. It was still the rainy season. We travelled to a spot on the main road nearest to my selection just eleven miles short of Chingola, and started to cut a track for four miles through the bush to reach my allotted farm and the spot I had chosen to camp. This was near the head of a stream and in a sentimental moment I called it Springhead Farm.

We pitched camp and started to build temporary pole and grass shelters. Slashing our way through the long grass that was over our heads, there was some confusion and we made camp at the wrong stream. After this false start, we had to move camp on to our own area, which I had eventually located. By this time the rains had stopped. So, I just put my bed up under a tree from which I hung a mosquito net, erected a grass shelter wall halfway round, built a fire with a twenty-gallon drum over it for hot water and a tin bath alongside it, positioned my wooden arm chair and table to give me a view of the distant hills, and started my independent bachelor life. I felt like a king taking his throne in his own domain. I had my two dogs with me, and felt very safe and secure in this virgin bush.

Our wedding had been fixed for the end of the year, so my first priority was a house. Brick-making was started—the big sundried type called Kimberly Bricks—while suitable trees were cut for timber and sawn by hand over a pit by two young sawyers. A house plan was made, simple and easy, foundations were dug, and soon we were on our way. When the planks had been cut, a very skilled carpenter was employed. His name was Leacha, and he made all the window frames and sashes, door frames and doors.

Poles were cut for the roof, lathes were stretched across them and the house was thatched. The floors were of beaten black anthill mud, and the walls plastered with more of the same after it had been sieved and mixed with sand. About the only things we bought were screws, nails, hinges, door locks and glass. The rest we cut or dug from the surrounding bush.

The loo was a long drop behind an anthill, and water was dragged up from the stream by two oxen in a forty-four-gallon fuel drum lodged on a forked piece of timber cut from a tree. It was all finished by the time the next rains came, ready for occupation and furnishing. Our furniture was made in the carpenter's shop at Hillwood, funded by wedding gifts of money.

But what of the farm? We cleared some land for our first crops, I bought a few cattle, started some poultry, and grew some vegetables. We were on our way, or so it seemed. Nothing was further from the truth.

I had succeeded in persuading the Trustees of my father's Estate to loan me some money. Why they agreed to do so, I cannot now fathom. I had no business plan, no budget plan, no farming plan. Above all, I had no idea of the fundamentals of business management or how to make the right investments to generate income, let alone build further capital. I was just cruising along, navigating by feel and inclination.

I achieved a lot, but to little purpose. I worked hard, very hard, but produced little. The ensuing ten years were a tremendous waste of energy but a massive learning curve. I can say now that nothing is wasted in life; it is all part of the mix out of which the rest of our time grows. At that time, I didn't know what I was doing, so I eventually fell flat on my face. And that is the truth. By the time I learned a few of the facts of business life, I was in so deep I had difficulty seeing my way out. Optimism is as bad as pessimism at times like that. As I have said, it was a long and painful learning curve, but perhaps I needed it.

However, those years were not all bad. Anne and I were married after Christmas 1950 in the Church at Kalene Hill Mission, which her Grandfather had established forty years previously. I was anxious to get back to our farm, so with the honeymoon over, we drove back to Chingola and together settled down to our new married life. It must have been tough for Anne, and I am now amazed as I write this at the extent of her love and loyalty as she came with me.

Although the farming and business part of our life was not that successful, we developed a happy home, acquired some very good friends and above all, four of our children were born during those ten years on our Springhead Farm. We learned a lot about married life, for which we had had no formal preparation; we raised our family in which Anne was the key factor by inherited instinct as well as from her previous experience in the orphanage, and we had some good and happy times.

It is all a long time ago, but I want to give a realistic picture of those early years. Incidentally, they were not that different from those experienced by many other young people who came to make a home and to farm in this country. But there were many pitfalls of which we were quite unaware.

Our farm was on the edge of what was then called Native Reserve, set aside for village dwellers but as yet unoccupied. From the bush signs, there must have been a lot of small game there at one time, and there were still quite a few animals around. Porcupine were evident and I lost my faithful dog, a cross Great Dane-Alsation, when he was hunting them and got quills in his head, from which he went blind. Bush pig were a plague to our crops, and we ate quite a bit of their meat. During the dry season, we were visited by elephant. Not many, just a few young bulls who walked along the edge of the bush within sight of the house as though they owned it, which of course they did, in their search of fruit from the trees. By this time, we had several Bull Terrier dogs, who became so excited at the sight of them one day that they rushed out to see the intruders off. One of the terriers, a pup we had bred ourselves, distinguished himself by rushing in and biting the hind foot of one young bull, and living to tell the tale. The elephant swung around on the dog who leapt backwards, falling on his back with his legs in the air, and the elephant's tusk drove into the ground between his back legs. This incident was witnessed by some workers who had never seen elephant before and had gone out to have a look from a safe distance.

As we progressed through the years, the pitfalls lying in wait for us began to take their toll. Beyond a learning curve, it became a steep, uphill road as we began to understand our weaknesses as well as our strengths, what we could do, and what we could not.

Among these pitfalls were the tsetse fly. I had no previous experience of these silent killers; unknown to us there was a pocket of bush near us where they flourished, and our cattle became infected. In their weakened state, these animals began to suffer from other diseases but did not respond when treated, and just died. I was mystified. Eventually we discovered the truth, and I treated animals showing signs of weakness. I learned to give treatments directly into the jugular of stricken animals, and managed to save a few. But the damage had been done and our herd, which was supposed to be growing in number, was depleted badly.

Maybe we gained a little wisdom in all this and from other challenges that we learned to cope with, but we definitely accumulated a lot of experience in the process. We learned about people too. "Up Country", as we called it, we had lived in rather a rarefied atmosphere consisting mostly of the missionary community of whom there were many, and the Lunda people who were of course predominant. We were now on what was known as the "Copperbelt", comprising a belt of copper mines stretching across the country for about one hundred miles. These mines, and the support system that grew up around them, were manned by very different types of people from different countries. There were the British of course, many from the mining areas of Wales, the North, and Cornwall. There were many South Africans, mostly Afrikaans people, whose language was spoken widely. Sweden, Norway, Yugoslavia, Greece, Australia and Canada were all represented. There were professional people like doctors and school teachers, experienced miners, technicians and artisans as well as those who came just for a job, whatever was going.

The mines were very prosperous, wages were high, and there seemed to be plenty of money. The town grew rapidly; large department stores and smaller shops appeared overnight, mostly run by middle European Jews. The Mining Company built well-equipped hospitals in which four of our five children were born. They were staffed with top medical people. Everything was done to keep the wheels of the mine turning and the copper churning out without a hitch. World prices were at an all-time peak. The streets were full of spacious American cars, and community life was vibrant.

Sport was a big thing, and the mines provided everything needed to keep their staff happy, from golf courses to rugby pitches. The Mine Club was a centre for all this, and its bar figured largely in people's thinking.

Many of the mines' expatriate work force had never had so much money at their disposal and spent it on high living as fast as it came in. Some lived on credit, while others carefully invested their income, lived wisely and later moved on to a more stable lifestyle. I suppose this was typical of mining communities because even at the best of times, there seems to be an underlying sense of uncertainty and insecurity. It's wonderful while it lasts, but it can collapse suddenly.

This was clearly illustrated when a nearby mine that had started with a flourish and great hopes, suddenly closed. Management called all the staff to a meeting one evening and informed them that, to their regret, the decision had been made to close the mine as from that hour. The cost of keeping the flood water down underground was just too great, and they were washed out. Hundreds of men were paid off the next day and went looking for new jobs, or just went back from whence they came, trailing their families with them.

Alcoholism along with fractured marriages and families were quite common in those mining towns, and featured significantly in this hard-working, hard-playing and hard-drinking community. These people were the expatriates, of whom very few had been raised in the country.

I have not mentioned the huge community of African people, from every tribe and part of the country as well as from Angola and the Congo. For every person with a job, whether on the mines or in the supporting services and surrounding homes, there were large numbers of their immediate and extended families and friends who left their remote villages to come and live with them, to experience the new type of life in the towns.

There was at that time very little cross-over between the two distinct communities, even in the facilities provided by the mines for these two classes of employees and workers. Hospital, clubs, sports facilities and shops were quite separate, and socialising between the two was just not done.

It was alongside this mining community that we lived, and frankly we were a bit out of our depth. With the lavish lifestyle we could not compete; we did not drink, socialise or play sport. We did not seem to fit, although we made some very good friends with whom we had good times and from whom we received valuable input. I did have contact at times with the farming fraternity further south, but it was limited.

It was while we struggled along that we began to realise that all was not well. Change was in the air. The African Giant was beginning to wake up, and the political unrest and aspirations began to invade even the mining world. While the Management appeared all-powerful, they were under constant pressure from distant Boards of Directors and shareholders to produce the goods. To do this they had to have a stable workforce, and this was controlled by the Unions. Two of them of course: one for white expatriates, and the other for the African workers who were in the majority.

I don't know about the latter, but the European Mine Workers Union was a closed shop; all mine employees in that category had to be members. They were now beginning to see danger signals, and their previously secure jobs were in jeopardy. Up to that point, any skilled jobs for artisans, machine operators and so on, were reserved for them. No African artisans would be tolerated, even though there were many who had been trained elsewhere and could now do the job. A clash was inevitable; it was just a matter of time.

Apart from that there was racial discrimination at all levels, which was historic and endemic. It was a recipe for upset as folk felt their privileged way of life, in fact their whole future, was becoming unstable, insecure and threatened. In the light of events it proved unsustainable anyway, and in the long run faded away. So much for our community.

As for ourselves, things did not go any more smoothly as the years passed. In our own home, we were happy, enjoying our family life and friends. Until one evening, when disaster fell.

For house lighting, we relied on paraffin lamps and candles. That evening, in the little bathroom, a curtain blown out by the wind caught on fire from a candle. Within minutes, the reed mat ceiling above it had also caught on fire; from there, with a great roar, the flames swept through the roof of the house. We were in the sitting room at one end of the house, our two babies asleep in their room at the other end. At the first sound, we dashed through into the bedroom. Anne, with her usual unhesitating actions, seized both children and ran for it into the surrounding bush. I grabbed a trunk of linen and backed out of the house, dragging it behind me.

We were so overcome with the smoke that it was some minutes before we recovered enough to take in what was happening. By that time, the house was ablaze from one end to the other, the flames and smoke rising high into the dark night, which brought our workers and their families rushing. But nothing could be done. The heat was immense as the flammable materials—thatch, ceilings, roofing, felt flooring, the lot—burned like a furnace fanned by the wind. Within an hour it was all just a smouldering heap.

Our home was gone, and all our belongings with it: the books that we loved; our set of china bought in London and meant to last us a lifetime had collapsed onto the floor as the china cupboard around in burned, every plate in the stack neatly cracked in half; our furniture, our clothes, even our two puppies who had rushed into the house for protection were burned to death. All we had was ourselves, our little girl and baby boy. It was bad enough, but it could have been a terrible tragedy. We and the babies were safe. What more could we ask?

Our one-ton truck had been parked away from the house so was untouched. We sadly climbed into it, and drove through the night to another farm nearby where Anne's sister Sheila and her husband, Henry, lived. We stayed there with them for the next few weeks, while we pieced our lives back together. Many expected us to call it a day and move onto something more lucrative. But we were not beaten, or at least we were not prepared to admit it.

Within weeks a new house had been planned and building started, this time with more permanent and fire-proof materials. We received support from friends who did all they could to help, not least by giving us a fancy and supposedly non-smoking fireplace built by a bricklayer friend from the mine. It smoked worse than any we have had before or since! Friendships made during those years were strengthened and have since stood the test of time. Somehow, we gathered all the materials, and within six months we had a roof over our heads again, although it was rather bare inside for a while. Our financial cupboard was even more bare. I had no choice; I had to get a job.

My first job was driving heavy earth-moving machinery, digging away the surface soil to a depth of almost two hundred feet so that the miners could reach the copper ore below. The work was for a contracting company; speed was the operative word, and it was all go. We worked shifts of twelve hours, one week at night, the next by day. During the day, we had a thirty-minute break for lunch and for servicing and fuelling the machines. During the night shifts, we had a fifteen-minute break for food. For the rest of the shift, it was driving flat out, night or day, hauling twenty-five ton loads of soil out from deep in the pit and climbing up onto a high spill, driving as fast as we could.

The machines never stopped except for service and from Saturday midnight to six o'clock on Monday morning. Nothing was spared—neither men nor machines—to achieve the set targets. It was, or could have been, dangerous. From six in the morning until six at night, and the next week from night to morning. There must have been twenty machines all going at speed in both directions; the roar of engines was deafening. But surprisingly, there were no collisions or accidents, although one man was killed when a machine reversed over him in the dark. One night, a driver hit a light pole causing at first massive sparks and then complete darkness as the great arc lights faded out.

Everything came to a sudden halt and utter silence, eerie after the rapid movement and ear-splitting roar of twenty machines. Within half an hour, however, the lights were restored and we were off again.

I worked this job for ten weeks and earned a lot of cash, but it was unsustainable work for a family man. Most of the operators lived on-site in caravans, while I had a fifteen-mile drive home. A kindly senior man on the Nchanga Mine eventually obtained a different job for me working as an operator in the copper refining process; also shift work but only for eight hours at a time. Recording chemical and electronic readings hourly, adjusting valves, walking around to ensure that all was working as per the specified needs, filling in forms of details, and drinking tea to keep awake—it was one of the most inactive jobs I have ever done. I would sooner have been driving. But needs must.

There was not a good atmosphere in the plant, or at least one I could relate to among my fellow operators. It was not a happy time for all of us, but Anne and the children were supportive. While working night shifts, sleeping during the day was very difficult for me; this was action time according to my inbuilt clock. Anne had to wake me up mid-evening and set me off to drive fifteen miles to start work at ten o'clock. It was an upside-down life, and I was not enjoying it. We managed to keep the farm work going between us, but it was inadequate for making any progress towards establishing a secure life. In fact, it was quite the opposite, just hand to mouth, but at least it kept the wolf from our door and provided for our immediate needs.

The *coup de grâce*, the fatal blow, did eventually come. A dispute that had been brewing for some time was finally declared between the Mine Management and the European Mine Workers Union. It was over "Job Reservation" when the Union challenged the Mine Management regarding their upcoming policy of moving qualified Africans into artisan categories and work that was previously reserved for European workers. The EMW Union and its members were threatened by this new policy, feeling that their long-term security was at risk. Which of course it was.

A Union meeting was called—compulsory, such was the power of the Union—and a vote taken as to whether or not to strike. Five voted 'Against', the rest voted 'For'. One of the 'Against' votes was an elderly man who, from his past experience, knew strikes never achieved anything. Another was a man I knew who always seemed to be against anything that others were for. Two of them I did not know, and I was the fifth. It was a funny feeling lifting one's hand high among several hundred other men to vote against what they had all voted for, but I knew the Union was wrong. I would be going against all my training, culture and instincts to give a 'For' vote.

Ten weeks of stalemate ensued. The mine stopped operating, salaries were no longer earned or paid, and it had devastating effects. There was no money to spend so consequently retail shops and businesses collapsed and closed down. Credit was no longer available for the miners' wives to buy necessities because there were no pay cheques to come at the end of the month. These highly-paid, high-living people were in trouble.

The atmosphere was tense among the previously happy-go-lucky communities across the Copperbelt, but most Union Members believed their cause was just. Of course, the mines kept paying the African mine workers, who had a wonderful time. Some were kept on for essential jobs of maintenance, but the banks of the Kafue River were lined daily with happy men fishing, and sports went on at their clubs on work days as well as weekends. They knew the tide was in their favour and they would win in the end. But it was the end of the Copperbelt as we had first known it.

The Management eventually won the day. They could see ahead and knew that the famous Winds of Change were coming, and that political changes were not far over the horizon. The British Colonial Office knew the same, and had little sympathy for the European Miners. It was tough for them, because many had served in the British and Commonwealth armed forces in the recent WW2, some with great distinction. They felt they were being let down.

It was the end for us too. I now had no income from my job, and had difficulty selling farm produce. I was owed money for produce supplied to one of the shops which had gone bust, and eventually got three shillings in the pound from the administrator when its affairs were wound up. The shop had been owned by a Lithuanian Jewish refugee who had walked into Chingola years before with a shoe on one foot and a carpet slipper on the other. He built two businesses, both of which went bankrupt that year, but he still left the country years later as a millionaire.

At this time Anne's Dad, Mr F., our respected Pa, had had a serious operation on his legs, done by his surgeon brother, to enable him to keep walking and mobile. He had been in great pain for quite a while from his damaged legs and war wounds, and while the operation relieved this pain he now became severely crippled. I visited him in the Government hospital, and sat by his bed chatting. He wanted to know how we were doing and I told him, the good and the bad. There was no point in doing anything else. He was quiet for a bit, and then asked if I would consider returning to Hillwood Farm to manage the cattle and farm for him, as it was now beyond him.

For me, this was an offer to escape from a pretty impossible way of life, one which neither Anne nor I were enjoying and which was going increasingly sour on us. For our own sake and the children's, we needed out. Beyond that, here was a chance to work at and carry forward something with which I was familiar, which I loved, which would give me a challenge and fulfilment and possibly a future. It was also something whereby I could recover my self-confidence, which I admit had been severely dented. Thank God, Pa still had faith in me. It certainly fulfilled our needs of the moment, and the prospect ticked the boxes in many other ways. Anne would be returning to her beloved home and familiar surroundings, we would have a secure home and more sensible lifestyle, and be near a school for the children. Above all, I felt Pa was not just being kind and helpful as was his nature, but he needed us, both of us. It felt good to be needed.

The long and short of it was that someone was found to take over Springhead Farm. He was a single man, a Swede who was a very skilled miner but who had had terrible personal problems that had cost him his family and his self-respect. He was a powerful, fine looking man; his African name was Simba, meaning "Lion", and it suited him well. Bravely, and with great determination, he had overcome his problems and wanted a quiet place away from the Mining Town life and into which he could invest his time and thoughts and have a home near his work. This suited him well. Sadly, two years later, he accidently fell down a new mine shaft he had just completed and was killed.

For us the die was cast. We now had something positive to do and could see the way ahead. Having paid all our debts, we packed up our belongings, and together with our children and pets (dogs, cats, and rabbits) we set out along the dusty roads up to Mwinilunga and Hillwood Farm to begin our new life.

This marked the beginning of a twenty year uphill but fulfilling journey. Together we established a better form of family life, for one thing, as the children grew. And I was able to recover my self-respect and re-establish myself as a serious operator in the farming world and community in which I had chosen to make my life.

9

FAMILY

"He saw his children."

Job 42:16

As I have said, the ten years we spent on Springhead Farm were not an easy time in many ways. However, it was there, in that environment and during those years, that we laid the foundations of our Family Life. It was of course the first ten years of our marriage, of making our own home, of establishing the norms and patterns of our daily life together, and overcoming the challenges and the give-and-take adjustments of sharing. We read somewhere that, "If two could live for the price of one, it would be fun, but it can't be done". That can be applied quite widely, way beyond the actual cost. But we were young, and we learned, though perhaps the hard way sometimes.

The one thing we were in total agreement about was that family meant *Family*. Both of us came from sizeable families; Anne had four sisters and a brother; I was also one of six: three boys and three girls. Further back in both our family trees this size family seemed to be the norm, but it was not just tradition we wanted to follow; we had our own agenda, and children were high on that. And so it was. During those ten years, four of our five children were born. As a start, we celebrated our first wedding anniversary with our first baby girl.

Anne had a school friend with whom she had made an agreement when they parted that they would both have daughters whom they would call Elizabeth Anne, sharing their own names. I was happy with that; Elizabeth was my Grandma Wyatt's name, and my sister's second name. As the time of the birth drew near, Anne's family took control. Her Uncle, who was a doctor, insisted that this first baby should be born under his oversight in the hospital where he was in control. So Anne's Mama arrived and took her off to be near-at-hand when the time came, and I was on my own once more.

The day arrived, but I was over fifty miles away, being redundant at that stage of events. My brother-in-law Henry, who had a phone and had been warned, drove across to see me and relay the news.

"Russ," he said, "I think you should go to Luanshya now, things are under way!"

So I went. When I arrived, Ma was well in control. Anne was dozing in the ward, and I was escorted into the nursery. There lay my first-born daughter, sound asleep, with a shock of dark hair and a very red face that bore no resemblance to what I had expected.

"No, that can't be the one," I said, and went and looked in several other cots around the ward.

Having seen what else was on offer I was very happy to come back to her, and even happier when the time came to take them both home, and settle in on our own. My own little family, I was very proud.

Our baby girl soon regained her looks, and quickly grew into a lively toddler with long, wavy hair. As she grew, Anne always talked to her in Lunda (her idea of baby talk) and she also had a young Lunda nurse girl who carried her around, played with her, and saw she was safe in our bush surroundings. Not surprisingly,

110

her first language was Lunda, and she spoke to me in broken English with a degree of condescension.

We managed to get the funds together—one hundred and twenty English Pounds—and took our daughter to the U.K. when she was nearly two years old. I wanted to introduce both Anne and her to my wider family. One day during our stay, I was holding her in my arms while talking to a farmer friend.

"You know what, Russ? You need half a dozen more to go along with that one!" he said in his bluff and forthright way.

It was not so long after that our only son was on the way, although in those days one had to wait and see. He was born in the Nchanga Mine Hospital, fifteen miles along rough dirt roads from our home at Springhead Farm. It meant a midnight drive when the time came; Ma was on the scene again to look after things at home, while I took Anne into hospital. Another of her girlhood friends called Audrey was waiting, as she was a nursing sister at the hospital. I handed Anne over to her care, and Audrey said, "Now leave her with me, and you go home," which I did.

As I walked into the house the phone (we had one by then) was ringing.

"You have a son!" exclaimed Audrey.

Wonderful, as easy as that!

We had planned to call him David but that very day David, the young son of one of our key workers, died of malaria. No ways could we use that name, so we settled for a good second choice after Anne's cousin, and Brian Walter Frank became the second arrow in our quiver. Liz was his second little mother, and he grew into the heftiest lad, a real weight to carry, but Anne was strong in the arm and coped well. One day an unknown but as usual friendly Afrikaans lady stopped her on the street in Chingola, patted Brian's tummy and said, "Gawd, your baby's fat, 'eh!"

We were delighted with the start we'd made in building our family. Within a couple of years, Sheila made her appearance. Another night-time trip to town, the bumpy ride over the rough road probably helping the process. We just made it, and again on my arrival back home to make sure the other two were okay, a phone call brought the good news.

We were by now getting quite used to our small family: meal times, bed times, the lot. I suppose broken nights, sicknesses and the rough and tumble of kids exerting their rights were a part of it all, but those are completely put in the shade by the fun times and funny doings of our offspring. At least we seemed to be doing something right.

For Julia's birth, we decided to move into town, renting a Mine house whose occupants were on leave. It was not a good idea really; the house was uncomfortable and smelt of cats, but it served its purpose. Anne was not too well after the birth, which made the new baby a bit fractious. But thankfully everything settled down again, and like the others nothing seemed to hold Julia back as she grew into toddler stage. When she was about two years old, we took our young family to the U.K. again, to attend my youngest sister's wedding among other things. By this time, Julia had developed a love of singing and could hit the right notes with ease and clarity. This she did from the depths of our pew in the fashionable London Church, clear and loud, to the astonishment of the lady soloist who was singing a special anthem. It was a musical wedding, and Julia added her bit.

There are so many little incidents I remember concerning our children, such as the day a porcupine had been digging up our potatoes and sadly had to be shot. It was lying on its back in repose, its powerful little paws stuck straight up in the air. Liz stared at it for a long time, and then leaned forward and gently shook its paw, in a sort of farewell.

Another amusing occurrence was at the local Show, where we were watching the horse-jumping events from the stands. All the competitors were having trouble with a jump quite near us made of conifer tree branches until Brian suddenly jumped to his feet and yelled, "I wish someone would move those blooming Christmas trees!" There was a roar of laughter from the other spectators, and Brian buried his head in his mother's lap, overcome with embarrassment.

Sheila was a very independent child. One day when we were shopping in a neighbouring town and she was supposed to be with Anne, she ran away. I caught a glimpse of her from a street-length away running diagonally through the traffic at a cross-road. When we were in the U.K., she fell out of the car onto the road, the result of rough-and-tumble of all of them on the back seat (seat-belts were not a feature in the cars of those days). The first I knew of it was seeing her reflection in the rear-view mirror, first rolling in the road, and then getting up and starting to run after the car. Not a tear, just a nasty cut on her forehead.

Julia simply contented herself by throwing her bottle out of the car window when she had drunk all her milk.

We are old now, and probably could not cope with little children day and night. But when our grandchildren were small they often came with their parents to stay, and sometimes we had one or two of them to stay alone for a while. We once had seven little boys under seven years of age staying in the house. We still delight in it when our grandchildren and great grandchildren come to visit, or we are able to go to see them. The total count of our direct descendants is currently thirty-one. We are so very rich in this, and have never regretted for one moment what we light-heartedly embarked upon so many years ago.

I cannot say it was all plain sailing. We had our times of great anxiety, not least the sorrow and risk of sending our children so far away to boarding school in different countries. Then, as they matured and went away for training and their work lives, it was hard to let them go. But we had to, hard as it was. We had made our lives independently of our parents, and they wanted to do the same.

Liz became a nurse, training in Durban and Cape Town, South Africa. Sheila went to college in Wales, completing practical secretarial and farm girl training. Julia trained as a Nursery Nurse in Reading, England, and Helen, our youngest, attended a business training college in the U.K. too. Brian chose the farming life, and spent three years working under a very focused and successful farmer in Zambia, before farming in his own right.

They all married, had their own happy families, and established themselves in life. It was only Brian and his lovely wife Gayle who lived near us for many years, with their three growing children. The rest were based in either South Africa or overseas.

It was at the height of all this and when everything seemed to be on track and going well, that tragedy struck. I will not go into details, but our only son suddenly died. He had not been feeling well one Saturday morning, had seen the doctor, gone back home and was watching rugby on TV with his cousin. He went through to the kitchen for a drink of water, collapsed on the floor, and was gone, all in a few minutes. He had a previous heart problem, and it could only have been that.

The next few days were a daze as the whole family gathered, flying in at short notice from around the world, including his two boys who came from school and university. We held a memorial for him in his own garden, attended by scores of his many friends, and surrounded by his wheat fields; a crop-spraying plane flew over us in salute to his memory. He had been known for his friendliness and generosity, and his fun-loving nature. Testimony was given to this, not least by the village folk from around, several of whom said to me, "He was our friend". And also by his farm workers.

He left a wonderful legacy in his three children and their mother who was just another of our daughters, and still is. He had worked so hard and with such skill in getting his farm productively efficient, and his first irrigated wheat crop, as yet un-reaped when he died, bore testimony to that.

The gap, years later, is still there. I had lost my father when I needed him most. Now I had lost my only son on whom I was beginning to lean, and who had been such a support to his mother and myself. We had to be strong for him, and his bereaving family, and take up where he left off, fulfilling our role as grandparents as best we could for them.

When I see his grandchildren now, growing so well and such fun, I can only think how he would have loved them, and what they are missing in not having known him. But the memory of his years is still alive and meaningful. He was a man of Africa. A skilled and experienced crop farmer, he was also a superb manager and a fair and respected employer of his farm workers, especially as he was fluent in two tribal languages. He also loved fishing and camping expeditions into the bush, where he took his children and taught them the rudiments and rules of bush life and conservation.

I quote a little poem, taken from the book *Out of Africa* by Karen Blixen and adapted by Brian's sister, Helen, to fit the occasion. It was printed on his memorial leaflet for the special gathering of all of us together with his friends some days after he left us.

> *"I knew a song of Africa—of the lion, and the African new moon lying on its back,*
> *Of the ploughs in the fields, and the sweaty faces of the farm workers—does Africa know a song of me?*
> *Would the air over the wheat fields quiver with the colour that I had on,*
> *Or the children invent a game in which my name was,*
> *Or the full moon throw a shadow over the gravel drive that was like me,*
> *Or would the fish eagles of the Zambezi River look out for me?"*

And so it was: the joys and anxieties, the fun and frustrations, the achievements and the tragedies, all are a part of family life and fulfilment. I repeat: how rich we are in this, both as things are now and with the memories of the past. The Psalmist wrote that God puts people together in families, and for very good reason. There is nothing more fulfilling or more secure than family life.

As a great man once said: "How does a family start? It starts with a young man falling in love with a girl. No superior alternative has yet been found."

What more does one want than that? And what better legacy can one leave behind at the end of the day?

10

FREEDOM

"Whatever your hand finds to do."

Ecclesiastes 9:10

Hillwood Farm is tucked away in the far north-west of this country, but within half an hour's drive of both the Congo and Angola borders. Remote as far as the rest of the country is concerned, it is central to the region. This was fine in early days when the only formality in crossing the borders was a cup of coffee with the Chef de Poste on the veranda of his villa, but it did present problems when things became more formalised.

The farm is also within half an hour's drive of the source of the Zambezi River, from where the tiny but sparkling start of this great river grows amazingly as it winds its way around the area before disappearing into Angola, then back into Zambia again to makes its placid way to Victoria Falls and the gorges beyond. It is a region of higher rainfall than most, the rainy season lasting longer and with heavy rainfalls. The climate is mild although it can be quite hot in September and October before the rains settle in to cool things down, and windy and cold in June, the winter month. Beyond all that, it is of course the Family Home, and as such the centre of family life and thinking, certainly as far as Africa is concerned.

It was into this location that Anne and I happily settled down, in our own house on the farm just five minutes' walk from its centre comprising the cattle pens, dairy, business stores and office. For the previous two years, our eldest daughter, Liz, had been living with Anne's parents so that she could daily attend the School across the Sakeji River. This school had been started by Anne's grandparents, the Doctor and his wife, in their retirement, especially for the children of missionaries. Our latest move meant we could be together as a family again. It was wonderfully relaxed after the pressures of the past two or three years, to be able to put our own home together in this place where we felt we could really become involved with a purpose.

My priority was to get a grasp on my new responsibilities on the farm and with the cattle, and to become involved in all that was going on. I was, of course, familiar with the lay-out and much of the work force, so had a reasonable start.

There were around fifteen hundred head of beef cattle beside the Jersey dairy herd, and the small stock in which Mrs F., now our Ma, had a hand in her own style. Unlike previously, when I was just involved in the daily work and routines, I was now more deeply involved in the management, policy and business aspects of the Company which Pa (Mr F.) had incorporated under his own name. I had to gain a clear view of what held things together and how it all worked. The primary asset were the cattle, which were a steady source of revenue, but the trading stores were the major contributor to cash turnover.

It was the cattle to which I first turned my attention. There were many herds of breeding cows, besides young breeding stock and steers. About half of the breeding cows with their calves were kept on the homestead and taken out daily to graze in the surrounding bush and green plains along the river and streams within the farm boundaries. The remaining herds were in strategically placed camps in the Chief's areas, as much as ten miles away, and grazed there. Routine work such as branding, dehorning and castrating calves, dipping and dosing for worms, all had to be brought up to date, and with a little organisation and input this was soon done.

The cattle were generally in good condition and in appropriately numbered groups. However, my immediate concern was the small number of calves born over the past two years. This, as soon became obvious, was related to the inadequate number of bulls. There was an urgent need to put this right. To this end, I took a long journey to the Southern Province where there were large beef herds from which I could source and buy young bulls. I took my son Brian, just turning eight years old, with me on the trip and we stayed with one of the last of the great cattle barons of the country in Mazabuka. He was helpfulness itself, a real gentleman whose great interest was his cattle, numbering about four thousand head at that time. I was amazed at his personal knowledge of each of his herds and individual cattle, and in those few days learned a great deal about application to detail.

We selected five bulls, two of which were Sussex, two South Devon, and one Afrikander. We arranged for these animals to be railed to Ndola shortly afterwards, and I headed for home to quickly return with our lorry, fitted with strong sides and a shade cover, to collect them there. We backed up to the rail truck at Ndola railway goods yard, and with some difficulty transferred them. The Sussex and Devon bulls were fairly quiet and easy to handle, but the Afrikander was excitable and prepared to defend his space. Once all of them were aboard and secure we had to get moving; timing was a factor and we had a two-day journey ahead. We also had to travel at night through certain areas because of the threat of tsetse fly, and therefore had to time the trip just right. At dawn, we pulled over into the shade of trees and slept through the day, having lit smoky fires up-wind of the lorry to keep the killer flies at bay.

I remember those bulls well, and they made a huge contribution to future calf crops at Hillwood. If I remember rightly, the percentage calf crop—that is the number of calves to the number of breeding cows—was about thirty percent the year I arrived. After the introduction of these bulls, with the cows on a rebound, the following year the calf crop was over ninety per cent.

With a little rearranging and planning, we soon had the cattle sorted into their right age groups and a working system of planned movement and upgrading in place. In doing this and working with the cattle I was able to familiarise myself with the cattle themselves, their herdsmen, and the areas in which they grazed. I soon had a clear picture of it all in my head, cattle on the ground and a more detailed system of recording. It was a pleasure to drive Pa out in the late afternoons to one outside camp or another that was accessible by road, to see the cattle as they slowly moved through the bush towards their night kraals as the evening came on.

It was evident to me that the structure and system of the cattle management, which had developed in the past under the hand of Mr F. as the numbers grew, was still intact. It just needed to be brought up-to-date as things had slipped a bit as his failing health limited his activity. He now seemed content, which gave me great pleasure and encouragement.

At that time, the Government as it was then had developed a scheme to encourage the building of beef cattle ranching. For every heifer raised to a certain age they paid a subsidy of five pounds per head. The heifers had to be of good quality, were inspected by Livestock officers and branded with a U on the left cheek. I felt we should now cash in on this, and contacted the right people whom I had previously come to know when on the Copperbelt. I pleaded the fact that in previous years no advantage had been taken of this scheme due to Mr F.'s ill health, and they agreed to stretch a point and take in animals that were really beyond the stipulated age. The whole operation went well; a team of men came, and we spent a few days going through all the herds of young female stock eligible for inspection. Every group was brought forward, from weaning to breeding age; nothing was turned down, the work was done, and it turned into quite a social event. The resulting cheque from the Government was a good boost to our finances.

On the last score, it became obvious as we moved into this new responsibility that the finances of the Company were not in very good shape. Over the years, Pa had built up a prosperous and continually growing enterprise: an amazing achievement in view of his limitations due to his war wounds and lack of experience when he started out. The place was in very good shape, and the fixed and liquid assets were strong. But times were changing. Better road communications had increased trading options for consumers, and their requirements were changing. Costs were rising too. In his failing strength, Pa had given considerable latitude to the management that had been in place up to that time. It became evident that, while trading and cash turnover had increased, financial management and control had been lax. Credit was now tight and working capital very limited.

I for one did not have a very good past record in financial management at that stage, but perhaps I had learned a little something. My brother-in-law Paul had even less experience than me in this area, but was financially conscious. Pa in his convalescence was finding the going tough, but we had to look at things as they were, and not bluff ourselves. The situation as it was would not go away, or even resolve itself on its own. There had to be positive action.

For a start, we listed all the creditors, most of whom were wholesalers within the country from whom we obtained trade goods and consumable supplies. Three companies were our major suppliers and creditors, and we openly explained things and came to terms with them as we needed supplies to keep us going. We then set ourselves to pay off all the smaller creditors as cash came in, and to pay cash for everything else we bought. It was a tight, uphill struggle, but we made it.

In the process, I developed an understanding of what should and must constitute a flourishing and effective business operation. Primarily, confidence and credibility in the operation had to be maintained, especially with both our suppliers and customers related to the trading part of the operation. Cash turnover had to be sustained. Integrity and open dealings with everyone were vital assets, which had to be guarded and strictly maintained. Material assets, such as the cattle herds, and the infrastructure, such as equipment and buildings and other fixed assets, had to be kept in good working order. We had to understand clearly the difference between accumulated debts which had to be overcome, and our established and agreed credit lines whether with the Bank or our suppliers and which were a normal part of ongoing business. Thirty- or even sixty-day credit lines on purchases made, especially for trading stock, were an enormous help to be used to the full but carefully controlled. Great care was taken to purchase only those goods for which there was a ready demand in the trading stores. Active and rapid turnover of stock giving a steady cash flow was the aim. Dead stock, or even items for which there was a very slow demand, were kept to a minimum. No expenditure was entered into unless there was a clear plan as to how and from where payment was to be made. And finally, the work force had to be kept in a positive frame of mind, active, and with full and effective awareness of what they were doing and what their contribution was to the whole. In other words, the maintenance of an active and progressive operation and the creation of a positive atmosphere at all levels.

This was exciting, and as we developed and pursued these criteria the situation gradually righted itself. I screened the cattle, especially breeding herds, and any unproductive cattle were eliminated and turned into cash. In due course, we found ourselves on firmer ground, and could begin to look ahead. That was another matter.

Once we got things moving in the right direction we began to relax a little, and those were happy days. From this remote place, the peak of the watershed, two large rivers ran in opposite directions—one north east and the other south west—eventually to spill into two great oceans. It was in this centrepiece of the geographical region, almost cut off from the rest of the country and the world by vast areas of sparsely inhabited bush, that we settled down into a routine in which families (our own and of those around) could enjoy one another and our beautiful surroundings. Those of our own wider family who had moved on and made their lives elsewhere, came from time to time to this Family Home to visit. Together we picnicked and swam, played and ate, talked and laughed, and the children grew strong, healthy and active in the open air. It was almost idealistic.

However, we were aware that there was a wider world, and there were family members and familiar places far away with whom we did not want to lose contact, and of whom we did not want our children to grow up in ignorance. So, drawing on our limited financial resources, Anne and I took our family of four and flew to the U.K. to visit family and friends, mostly mine, and experience a different world. Once there I was rather taken aback.

Things had changed in England since the war and post-war years I had left behind me originally, and even from the visit we had made in 1952. Folk seemed to have forgotten the war with all its challenges. There was a prosperity and security in these new years of plenty, and a standard of living I had never experienced, even pre-war. In the words of the then British Prime Minister, they had never had it so good. Compared to the simple and constrained lifestyle back home and our necessary careful watch over expenditure, it was a bit shattering. Had I made a right decision in leaving my homeland in the first place? Should I consider bringing my little family back to England and making a new start in this prosperous setting?

Our old family home, Pigeon House Farm, had been sold for a pittance (so it seemed to me) and much to my sorrow. But it did not seem to have affected the lifestyle of the rest of the family. While we, even on this holiday, were having to count every penny, these limitations did not seem to affect them. It was very unsettling for me.

However, we caught up with family, attended the wedding of my youngest sister, and had a seaside holiday with some of the family in South Wales. This was much to Anne's joy, as it was a place where she and her siblings had gone as children. Mother was in good health and active, though did not seem to be doing anything much other than living alongside and enjoying the rest of her family.

I am not sure that we all enjoyed that trip, but it did strengthen U.K. family ties. I think we were all glad to get back to Hillwood and settle once more into our routine as well as perhaps our simpler and more familiar life. It was our home, and with our dog and cats, rabbits, garden, and naughty monkey, it was a happy place, and life was full and meaningful.

Talking of pets, that monkey came into our life one unexpected day. The children came into the house carrying this tiny little thing in their cupped hands, crying and asking me to buy it off a man who was offering it for sale. Obviously, it was new born; its umbilical cord was still wet, and no doubt its mother had been hunted and shot just after giving birth. I thought that its chances of survival were slim and then we would have more tears. Nevertheless, under pressure and in a weak moment, the shilling or two involved were handed over for what I thought was a poor investment, tears were dried, and I waited for the inevitable. But I had not reckoned with Anne. She, with her great compassion even for the smallest thing in need, applied all her expertise and care. Aided by a tiny baby's bottle, warmed and diluted milk, a blanket, hot water bottle, and a dolly's bed, every care was lavished upon this tiny thing, and within days it was hopping around from first dawn on the kids' beds until late at night, as bright and at home as it could be.

Of course, it grew in size and mischief, but was constantly forgiven, and it gave great enjoyment. It played on Liz's bed, bit Julia, and clung to Sheila's neck for protection.

"No Daddy, you're not to smack him!"

Eventually it had to be restrained, and was tethered by a long, light chain to a tree up which it could climb to sit in its little weather-proof house, surveying the world around and planning its next moves. It soon became an escape artist, and would come over the house roof, swing down the creeper and, choosing its moment, jump down onto the breakfast table on the veranda, grab some toast, dip its hand into the butter or sugar, and was gone up the nearby tree before we could stop it. There it would eat its spoils while defiantly staring and making faces at us, and dodging anything we could throw at it.

The initial investment made in its purchase was nothing compared to the total running cost in wear, tear and maintenance. But it was fun. For our youngest, Helen, it was a faithful companion when the others had gone to school. She carried it in a cloth on her back just like the local women carried their babies, even as she rode her tricycle up and down the road. Then it graduated to sitting in a basket in front.

Eventually, when its teeth grew, it really became too dangerous to have around, and we had no choice but to release it in the bush where it could meet up with its own kind. Relief on the part of some, tears on the part of others, especially Sheila who had inherited a large portion of her mother's compassion for the underdog. The survival chances of tamed monkeys, or any tamed wild life which have been raised in company with humans, is poor when returning to their own habitat, but we very much hoped it made it.

On another occasion, a man cycled along the road at the back of our house with a young duiker tied on the back of his bicycle. The children saw it and ran outside, our trusty dog, Trudy, barking alongside them. The man took off at speed, the duiker fell off, and the children picked it up and carried it home. Although alive, it had been injured and could not stand. We nursed it for a day or two, and although it ate and drank it would not even try to stand. Helen and Trudy used to lie on the grass beside it; it did not struggle, seeming glad of the company. It was heart-breaking for the kids, but we had to put it down as there was no future for this beautiful little creature.

The local people seemed to have no heart for wildlife; they were just a source of meat and were trapped or hunted and killed whenever opportunity offered. Hunters would imitate the call of a baby duiker in distress, using a sort of whistle made from a piece of grass. If there was a mother in the vicinity she would hear, think it was her own hidden baby and rush towards the sound, only to be shot.

Dogs have always been a part of our lives. Trudy, a lovely Alsatian we had rescued from the streets of Chingola where she had been abandoned, was a much-loved pet. Although she was trained to walk on the leash, she was never tied and ran free. She was very obedient, a natural feature of this breed and almost self-taught. She was defensive of the family, watching over them with care, but never vicious or bad tempered. Her endless energy and strength was amazing. She would run behind my bicycle as I went miles out in the early morning to see cattle, only returning home for a late lunch. Having run anything up to twenty miles, Trudy was still ready and barking for a walk with the kids after tea.

I must mention a very special part of these years: the arrival of our youngest daughter, Helen. We had planned a good-sized family, regardless of expense so to speak, and her arrival rounded it off. Anne was healthy, we were still young, and the children we felt were the natural outcome of our love and life together, regardless of other limitations. Most of our baby kit had been worn out by the other four, and we now had to finance a lot of new stuff. Not easy, but there was a way. A minister in the Government, in an effort to bring different ethnic groups together, offered a reward to any expatriates if they would learn a local language and pass a set examination. This was a gift, and Anne sat the senior Lunda exam, I sat the junior one, and we both passed. I think both of us knew more Lunda than the oral examiner, and the written part went okay too. The result was a cheque from the Ministry of Finance for the princely sum of eighty pounds, fifty for Anne, thirty for me, which bank-rolled the purchase of all the new kit we needed for our fifth baby.

When the arrival date approached, Anne went to stay at Kalene Mission to be near the hospital where there was very experienced medical care, and where she herself had been born. Everything went well, and our nine-pound baby daughter arrived in due time. A few days after the birth, a missionary lady called by to see her. She had known my own family back in the U.K. for many years, and laughed loudly when she saw this contented little mite.

"Another little Wyatt for sure!" she exclaimed.

Helen was such a joy, and we spoiled her a bit I think. I do know she seemed to spend more time in our bed at night than in her cot, shielded from the danger of my squashing her by Anne's protective arm. She smugly snuggled down and slept soundly, and argued loudly when any attempt was made to return her to her own bed.

A young girl called Katy, daughter of the cattle Foreman, asked to help with her and became not only her nurse-girl but also her companion, friend and protector and very much a part of the family. In the early stages, Helen spent many hours tied on the back of this strong young girl in the traditional and comfortable style. Katy came early each morning, but instead of washing nappies and doing other chores she joined Helen's older sisters in their bedroom before they were up, and cries of fun would ensue as they played Snakes and Ladders on the bed.

As I said, we were a happy family.

11

SMOKE IN MY EYES

"For here have we no continuing city."

Hebrews 13:14

"If they had been mindful of that country from whence they came out, they might have had opportunity to have returned."

Hebrews 11:15

To go back to animals, there were hunting laws in place in the country, but they were largely ignored, certainly in these parts. Hunting licences were obtainable but there was little chance of a check-up on what was actually killed, or even wounded and left, which was usually way and above the number allowed.

A few men of local standing had 12 bore shot guns for which cartridges could be bought under permit ranging from SG, a heavier shot for animals like bush buck, through to number five bird shot. Most of the shooting was done with a flint lock gun, an ancient weapon such as was used in the Crimean war and earlier. To prime them, gunpowder was stuffed down the barrel together with a wad and slugs, which were often made from

127

old bolts and nuts, and detonated by a hammer released by the trigger and striking a live cap. They went off with a tremendous bang, giving out a great cloud of smoke. Occasionally the barrel split and was, illegally, just welded or brazed up again. I once met a hunter from down on the Kabompo River called William who used to shoot buffalo with one of these dangerous weapons.

Enterprising men could and did manufacture their own guns occasionally, using a piece of strong pipe for the barrel and spring steel powered by a strip of car tyre inner tubing. This, of course, was highly illegal under a manufacture of firearms act but the nearest law enforcer was fifty miles away.

I had been made an Honorary Game Warden, but any efforts I made to instil the idea of even recognising game laws, let alone obeying them, was not met with favour locally, even by the Chief. So, I handed in my badge as it led to some embarrassing confrontations and bad feelings.

The winds of change were blowing even in this remote area, and right across Northern Rhodesia the call among the people was for "Freedom". Basically, what that really meant was an end to rule by the British Colonial Office, and the election of their own leaders to govern the country.

Two political parties came into being in Northern Rhodesia, and there was much harsh rivalry between them that led to in-fighting and even deaths. Feelings were running high, and emotions went out of control at times. This was the real part of the "Fight for Freedom"—a fight for power and control—and the Police of the time were caught in the middle sometimes, trying to keep the peace and save lives. They had to be harsh at times to achieve this, which did not help. This was how I saw it at the time. Perhaps not many would agree with me now, as they may well have a different perspective.

Zambia has many tribes, each with their own history and language. In past generations, there had been some rivalry and even enmity between some of them. They had their differing stories and customs, and all this had an influence. "One Zambia,

One Nation" was a political slogan on many lips, but not always a reality in their inner thinking.

There were differing agendas too, as there were non-Tribal power points like the Labour Unions, the Civil Service workers, and so on. These had been influenced by external forces ranging from the University types who made up the Colonial Civil Service, through to Socialistic and Labour movements, and even Communism.

It was difficult for those of us who were on the ground not to get encumbered with all this, as our future was at stake too. Sometimes, relations were strained as what might be said or not said could be misinterpreted. There was a lot of hot air talked on all sides, which did not help either.

The transition, when it came, was well handled on the whole and as a result of a "One Man One Vote" day, the strongest and most influential party won the election. Northern Rhodesia became history and Zambia a reality as its new and colourful flag was ceremonially raised. The Federation of Rhodesia and Nyasaland also ceased to exist, and our Federal Passports were no longer valid. We were not eligible for Zambian passports by birth, so we reverted to British. Nonetheless, on that one special day, as residents and Federal Citizens we were eligible to vote, and so we did. That story is worth telling as far as was our part in it.

As I remember the sequence of events, it had been agreed at a conference in London between the British Government and our Political Aspirants that for a start there should be "One man, one woman, one vote". Then, under the new regime that would reflect the will of the people, and with new leaders, the next step could be decided.

The date was fixed and voting day came. Excitement was high. Our local polling station was at Chief Ikelenge's capital six miles from the farm, and throughout that morning news reached us of the doings and the crowd there. Many of our workers had taken the day off; they had heard that voting was from six o'clock in the morning until six o'clock in the evening. Some thought it was going to be a long day and they did not want to miss a moment of it. I felt that, while all must be given the opportunity to vote, if we released the dairy workers and other stockmen to go, their normal afternoon work would remain undone as that would be the last we would see of them that day.

So straight after lunch, Anne and I took the small truck and accompanied by these essential workers who had all piled in, we drove out to the polling station to try our luck, hoping that we could bring at least some of them back home with us. And of course, we would vote ourselves. As we drew near, we could hear the racket. Surrounding the Community Hall—now the Polling Station—was a yelling crowd of aspiring voters about twenty yards deep. They were pushing, shoving, shouting, and being pushed and shoved themselves forward and back, as they all jostled for position.

As we arrived, a clerk from the District offices recognised us and came across, greeted us warmly and asked if we had come to vote.

"Yes, we all want to vote."

He was delighted and most welcoming. But our question was, "How?"

His confident reply was, "No problem, just line up behind me."

This we did, Anne holding my belt and the others behind her. Our good friend then set off into the crowd, blowing his whistle and beating his way through the crowd with a baton of rolled up documents. They parted a bit to allow us through, and we snaked our way along behind him, battered a bit on each side mostly by women with howling babies on their backs; they kindly tried to make way for us but were pushed back into us by the pressure of the crowd around. All very close and friendly!

Eventually, we reached the hall doors safely. These had been completely broken off their hinges by the pressure of the crowd and were being propped up by sweating Chief's Messengers. The Chief himself was there trying to keep order, his deep, strong voice now reduced to a mere squeak. He received us in his usual courteous manner, apologised for the chaos and ushered us inside. Here, comparative peace reigned but excitement was still high.

It was a change from the crowd outside, and we were politely escorted through the system.

First, we had to dip our thumbs into a bottle of red ink, a bit watered down by now, to make sure we did not vote twice. Our identities were carefully recorded (there was no voters list, it was all-comers from wherever) and we were given voting papers. Candidates were identified by small figures like crowing cocks or the like, for those who could not read. Next, we visited the voting booths, which were looking a bit worse for wear by now with heavy use. There were queues at every stop; every move was carefully supervised to make sure we did it right, and there was not much privacy. It did not seem to matter who we voted for; the big thing was to vote.

Eventually our votes were cast, but what now? How did we get out? Where was the exit? No problem, we were told again; provision had been made. We were kindly ushered to the far end of the hall where there was a window just large enough to get through, and two strong men to assist. Anne and I were still fairly athletic, and with their help we were heaved through the window and into the welcoming crowd outside. Those outside happily reached up, received us, and set us on our feet but we were on our own now except for the crowd who seized us and propelled us to the rear, not unlike swimming against a strong current with the waters parting to let us through. We stayed on our feet by a miracle, and made it, laughing, to calmer waters. We had done our bit and voted, and now were free to go.

What struck us was the tremendous atmosphere of good will and understanding all round. This was a great day, and everyone was out to make the most of it. The chaos and uproar was a part of the process; we were all in it together, and everyone was enjoying it to the full. After all, it was one-man-one-vote, and who could fault that? It was a day to relish and remember. We made it back to our vehicle, and with our essential workers made our way home.

One of the gardeners, due to the confusion in the hall, had joined the wrong queue and before he had a chance to protest and with his voting paper still in his hand, he was heaved out through the window.

"What do I do with this now?" he asked when we got home.

"Keep it safely," we said. "It may come in useful one day."

One vote lost although proof that he had done his best. It made no difference to the outcome, which had been pretty obvious. Independence from the rule of the British Colonial Office was on its way.

That was the only time either Anne or I have ever voted, as thereafter we were no longer eligible.

* * *

In a democratic vote numbers count and we, as part of the expatriate community, now became a clear minority in a foreign land. Among those with whom we worked and lived, it had little effect. While we were dependant on them they were also dependent upon us, and we stuck together. Further afield, however, there were great changes. Where previously the expatriate community had had the advantage of skills which gave privilege and position, these now quickly eroded away, and in some cases, became almost a liability.

Education and technical training of national Zambian men and women had been going on steadily for years in all areas, and there was now a yearning on their part to benefit from their achievements and enjoy the income and lifestyle which they perceived as the due outcome and reward. It was not as simple as that, but that was how they saw it. Many people from other countries who had made this their home could not cope with this new development, and a large part of the expatriate community packed their bags and left.

It was an unsettling time and many talked themselves or were talked into leaving when in fact they would have been wiser to stay. Two major issues other than income-earning jobs, security, and a comfortable lifestyle were a legitimate concern: health care for the whole family and education for the children. The new Government's policy was to open the existing and vital facilities to everyone, and this put enormous pressure on them. The departure of qualified teachers and medical staff from the country did not help, and inevitably standards could not be maintained. For us and many others at that time, there seemed no alternative but to send our children out of the country for education. In fact, many of the new leaders in Government and other areas did the same thing. The alternative was to leave ourselves, which is what many others did.

Transition, especially when accelerated, can bring about serious difficulties for all. The massive anticipation in place on the part of the main part of the population did not materialise. The majority were still poor, their lives were still lived in the same manner; good jobs were limited and in fact, initially, they decreased. The sad fact was that little had changed other than for a favoured few. But still, Zambia—as we must call it now—was much better prepared for this freedom for which they had yearned than our two neighbours, Congo and Angola.

Angola's bid for freedom developed into a bloody war between the Colonialists and the main population. Congo seemed to achieve their independence overnight as the Colonial power suddenly opted out and this deteriorated into army mutiny, and a civil war, which seem to rumble on even today. In 1960, we witnessed first-hand the massive and heart-breaking panic evacuation, almost stampede, of foreign workers and residents from the Congo, mostly by Belgian nationals. As the mutiny flared, they fled their homes overnight with what they could pack into their vehicles, and set out for the Zambian border along every road and bush path available. The roads leading into the Copperbelt towns along the border were jammed with lines of vehicles several miles long as the harassed immigration officials tried to regularise the entry into Zambia of these people whose language they could not speak. Zambia was a haven of refuge in comparison to the boiling pot they had left.

But what of us? Our family were growing up; Liz was ready for secondary school and Brian not far behind. We had to look ahead. What should we do? At that time, we had missionary friends from New Zealand with whom we shared our problem. They were kindness itself; in fact, the father of one of the young ladies wrote offering us a home and job on his farm. We studied the ways of that country, talked about it with the children, looked at ways and means, and even booked berths on a ship, as there was now a two-year waiting list. But New Zealand was so far away!

An alternative was to take the family to the U.K. Our financial resources for establishing ourselves there were nil, but maybe the family would help, and it was my home country. This option we had to explore, and it was decided with agreement all round that I should go there to do just that. Anne bravely stayed with the children; they continued in school and she helped in the business at Hillwood while I spent five months moving among family and familiar places in the U.K., trying to see where we might fit and survive. It did not help that it was a very cold winter. I stayed with Anne's sister Sheila and her husband Henry Rudge on their farm near Ross-on-Wye, and helped where I could while there. I enjoyed the physical daily work on the farm, and found that my early learned skills were still there to draw on. But that was not leading anywhere.

Only one opening presented itself, and this was in a very prosperous company owned by my second cousins in the West of England. It was to take charge of a branch located in Cornwall of the stock-feed manufacturing business they had started for the distribution of farm animal stock feed, mostly an administrative and sales job. My friend and cousin Ray was very keen, as it would free him to return to the Company head office in Somerset. But I had misgivings, why I didn't know other than a strong feeling that this was not my scene. After much heart-searching, I was convinced my scene was in Africa.

So, to the consternation of all, I made a rapid decision; we could not procrastinate any more. I booked my flight, packed my bags, turned my back on the country of my birth, and returned to my family and what really was my familiar home. Incidentally, two years later, my cousins sold their company to a multi-national group, and if I'd been there I would probably have been out of a job. Who says Godly guidance in whatever form is not a factor in our lives?

Other factors now came into the equation, and became very evident on my return. Over the past six years, we had helped set Hillwood back on a secure footing, but where did we go from there? Between Anne's brother and sister-in-law and ourselves, there were eight children to educate, and Ma and Pa to be provided for in their latter years. The present level of business and income was insufficient to provide for all that. There was a need to expand the operation and generate more income.

The salary I was drawing, appropriate while the business was getting back on its feet, was now quite inadequate for our growing needs; I had cashed in my life insurance to pay school fees and we had no other resources. We had to look at the bare facts, which were now staring us full in the face, but there came about a divergence of view among us. The older generation were content for things to stay as they were. Understandably they could not cope with even the idea of expansion; they had done their bit so well, but their day was done. Not so easy for me to understand was the lack of vision other than for the status quo on the part of our own age group. And that is what carried the day.

To cut a long story short, Anne and I had to face the inevitable and look elsewhere. Where to and to do what were the questions that disturbed our sleep at nights. Liz had now started her secondary education at the top school in the country, far away in Lusaka; it took two whole days to get there by road in our small car. We were stumped. Farm management jobs in Zambia were now scarce as farmers either abandoned their farms or sold them to aspiring Zambian farmers. Should we go to New Zealand? Our ship passages were still booked and Anne's cousin, a doctor, had emigrated there and encouraged us to join him. And what about Australia? But we had no contacts there.

Once again, I felt I was at the end of the road. Anne was so supportive and confident, or if she wasn't (this was her loved childhood home) she never showed it. Her unwavering support and her assurance that God had a plan for our lives whatever may happen, held us together in our spirits and daily lives. And it certainly motivated me.

I knew I had to put Hillwood behind me. I loved the place, the work, and all it offered in so many ways. I had worked hard in helping to get it going again in the order it used to be when I had first known it, and I was satisfied in our having succeeded at that. But I had a family to care for and I must not let them down.

Once more I set out to explore, this time within the country. My journey took me to Lusaka, and into the office of a tough and very competent Yorkshireman who was the Chief Animal Husbandry Officer for the Government. And so began another chapter in our lives.

On board ship, en route for Africa.

Hillwood House, Anne's family home. A painting by Anne's Aunt, Kitty Fisher

Anne, as I first knew her

Anne's Mum and Dad, Ethelwyn (nee Marks) and ffolliott Fisher, on the front steps of Hillwood House

With Anne: our young days

Anne, on the banks of the Luakera River, a favorite picnic site

Our wedding day, 28 December 1950

Nzewu, a skilled hunter. He couldn't read a book, but could read bush signs without pause in his swift and silent walk

Sawulu: A knowledgeable cattle foreman, with whom I worked and from whom I learned much in my early years in Africa

The Government Ranch (Kitwe Ranch): skilled Tonga horsemen collecting cattle from out of thick bush

Working with cattle, often a dusty job

With a group of ranch breeding cows, recognizable as individuals to me

*Our country: pedigree Sussex heifer against a backdrop of
Chillongoma Hills, Kapanda*

Sussex stud cows, Kapanda

Our Homebred Jersey cow: Champion on Show

12

THE WAY AHEAD

"He went out, not knowing whither he went."

Hebrews 11:8

Our country was now moving steadily and purposefully into a new era although the overall structure, at least for the time being, remained much the same. It was simply a case of different people calling the shots. Many of the previous personnel who had been at Government Department level remained the same; some were moved up a notch or two to help steady the ship as the new politicians familiarised themselves with what it really means to be at the helm and direct the country, especially as they introduced a new focus.

At expatriate resident level, there was much unrest and many were unprepared for the future, whatever it might bring. Their minds turned south or overseas, and many of them upped stakes and left. This group included farmers, who are usually the most stable part of any population. Commercial farms were being sold well below their value, some even being abandoned altogether.

Others were sold for the value of the cattle on them, and then the cattle sold for slaughter.

A few enterprising people were cashing in on the situation and buying up land, confident of the future or just taking a gamble. Zambian leaders as well as business and professional executives took over vacant farms; in some cases, due to their not having any farming experience, these lay rather dormant and unproductive while others made good progress.

In this re-adjustment of larger commercial farming in Zambia, the proportion of the national cattle herd owned by commercial farmers and ranchers was in danger of being reduced beyond recovery. The tribal and traditionally owned cattle, though far greater in numbers than those on commercial farms, were at that time making only a limited contribution to the fresh meat consumer market. They were regarded mostly by their owners as a wealth asset and hedge, and as draught animals. However, there was a growing urban population that needed to be fed. This tricky situation was quickly spotted by the Animal Husbandry section of the Department of Agriculture, and just as quickly and inspirationally, they came up with a plan. It was into this situation that I walked in Lusaka, mid-1966.

The visionary proposal of the Government Chief Animal Husbandry Officer was to take over abandoned farms or suitable vacant land, establish State-owned ranches, and buy up all the breeding cattle as they came onto the market. A cattle-purchase structure was already in place as part of the Cold Storage Board and they proposed to bring that on board. The World Bank was being touched for the necessary funding, the Lands Department came alongside in procuring land, and all was set for action. Recruitment of field management staff commenced while a head office and the administration structure was set up. It was all go.

There were two provisos: one from the World Bank requiring that they appoint their own man as General Manager, which they did; and the other from the Politicians requiring one ranch to be established in each Province across the country, which happened.

It had been my vague intention just to pay a courtesy visit to my contacts in Animal Husbandry as part of my exploration mission. I had no knowledge then of what was going on. My Yorkshire acquaintance, Bernard, Chief of the Department, and his colleague Peter, were in conference at the time. They broke off when I arrived, welcomed me in their usual friendly way, and listened to my story. I didn't realise they weren't just being polite. They had both travelled widely to New Zealand, Australia and the U.K., and were not encouraging to me on that score.

"With nearly twenty years of experience in Africa behind you, why move away to unknown parts? You may cope with Australia, but what about your wife?"

Good point. They then outlined to me their plans to rescue the cattle industry, and there and then offered me a part in it, to take on and develop one of the proposed ranches, and I could even choose which Province I would like to go to (except the Northern Province where an appointment had already been made and things were underway). Amazing! They gave me a list of properties and areas they had already taken over.

"Think it over," said Bernard. "Go and have a look at these, and let us know."

It took some thinking about I must admit, but there were possibilities here. Was this the way ahead for us? It certainly would be a resolution to our search for a sustainable future without the upheaval of leaving the country and re-locating elsewhere. Even more importantly, we could not only continue in the life and work with which we were familiar, making a contribution to the country to which we had strong attachments, but we would also be close to our wider family and familiar friends. We had to take it seriously.

For a start, Anne, the children and I drove down to the Southern Province, talking over the proposition as we went. We were in this as a family and it had to fit. Our immediate purpose was to visit the first property on my list, which was also the closest. It was near Monze and having found the entrance road, we drove in. We were in for a shock. As we made our way slowly along the farm road, the rank grass on either side towered over our car. After about a mile or so we came to a dilapidated thatched farm house and unkempt, overgrown gardens. An elderly man was sitting by a fire on the veranda. He was cautious at first, but made no objection when I said we had come to have a look.

I walked around the house and across to the barns, workshops and cattle kraals, or at least where they had once been. I stared at the debris of what remained of it all. It was a depressing sight. The buildings and cattle kraals were all falling down and overgrown with head-high grass. A day-time bush fire with a strong wind behind it would have completely wiped out these remains of what had been the centre of a once-active farm. It seemed beyond recovery, and would require a totally fresh start all round. It could be done, I knew, and eventually was by someone else, but it was not hard to reach the conclusion that this was not for us.

Nothing about the place attracted us, either as a farm or a home. Nor did any possibilities immediately spring to mind as to what we could do to make this a viable operation. This was unusual for me as on the spur of the moment I can normally come up with at least a few ideas and possibilities. Added to that, it was in an area and district with which I was totally unfamiliar. We would be strangers here, both among the few remaining farmer neighbours, and among the local people from whom a workforce would have to be drawn.

I walked back to the car and told Anne what I thought. She, with her usual clarity of mind and observation, had already come to the same conclusion, without even getting out of the car. We had drawn a blank. I climbed in beside her, backed around and prepared to drive away, but as I did so, the old man came to life. He ran towards the car, beckoning me to stop. He wanted to talk.

"*Bwana*," he said, "Are you going away? Are you not coming here to live and make this a farm again?" He had seen our lively family and the possibilities of things coming to life again.

"No," I said, and his face fell.

"Two years ago, my boss left," he went on. "He sold the cattle, took the tractors and just went, taking his family with him. They have never come back. I have waited for him to come; I have tried to look after the place but I can't do it on my own. And he never comes. Won't you come and be my new boss?"

That was fifty years ago but I have never forgotten the pleading look on that craggy old face, the look of desperation. Nor have I forgotten the tragedy of that place, a situation repeated a thousand times across Africa as the winds of change blew—a gale in some places—and people at all levels saw their lives and the world they had known disappear, whatever its shortcomings might have been. The world in which they had lived and been secure had crumbled about them beyond their understanding, leaving them stranded and without apparent hope.

We returned to Lusaka and the Animal Husbandry office.

"That farm is not for us," I told them. They weren't surprised, and had an alternative.

"Well, what about this?"

The outcome of their second offer was that I joined the Zambia State Ranches operation and became the manager of a seventy-thousand-acre ranch in the Copperbelt Province of Zambia. That sounds grand and a big deal, but at that stage the proposed ranch was just a vast area of un-surveyed and undeveloped bush land, with just a small residential holding in one corner on the banks of the Kafue River. We returned to Hillwood, told the family of our plans, and I wound up my work there. Having made the decision, we were anxious to get moving into this new adventure.

* * *

This was the honeymoon period of the new State of Zambia, quite difficult to appreciate all these years later. All we wanted and needed for this new project was there for the asking. Funds were available, requisition orders were the key, and Government Stores were the fairy godmother.

While Anne and the children packed up at Hillwood, I started the ball rolling in our new venture. I took possession of a Land Rover vehicle from Government workshops, drew camping gear and basic equipment from the Stores and, guided by a Government survey officer, drove out to the site, crossing the wide Kafue river on a long steel and concrete bridge, known as Smith's Bridge after the man who constructed it.

We wound our way along a track through the bush for about four miles until we came to a stream. Here I chose a camp site and we made camp. I had one Lunda man with me from home called Mutifu, a very energetic and supportive man who, thoroughly at home in this situation, quickly sorted out the camp and we settled down together for the first night. I told him we needed workers, and the amazing African bush communication system went into action. I was hardly prepared for the rapid response.

I woke in my little one-man tent before dawn the next day to a shuffling and murmuring sound all around me. What was that? I pulled on some clothes and crawled out into the semi darkness. There, sitting quietly in the bush on all sides around the camp, was a crowd of men, scores of them, silent and patient. As I stood upright so did they, all staring at me expectantly. I called Mutifu.

"What's going on?"

"You wanted workers," he said. "Here they are."

We were underway.

The planners had already produced maps of the area so surveyors came and marked out roads and fence lines, cattle handling sites and housing areas; in no time at all we began to make access roads, cut fence lines, burn bricks and build workers' houses. Speed was called for as the buyers were already locating cattle and wanting to consign them to us. Most of my experience in Africa had been in utilising the plentiful man power and their specific skills, and this came into play. Soon, there were three gangs of thirty men each cutting and forming roads through the area, forty miles of them. Pit sawyers produced two-inch planks from trees cut on-site for cattle handling pens; hardwood poles were selected and cut from the bush for the kraals, and bricks were hand-made in moulds and burnt in great kilns. Lorry-loads of fencing materials arrived on site and fencers were trained and set about enclosing paddocks.

In all this, I was supported by two men with whom I had previously worked. The first was Fulayi, a tall man who ran everywhere and could outwork any of his fellows; he was a daunting fighter when roused, but when managed and directed was invaluable. The second was Sawulu, an experienced *kapitawu* or foreman and cattle-man. We had previously worked together a lot; he had his weakness but possessed a wealth of knowledge and bush craft, and was a good authoritarian. (His son from a late marriage, Kwenda—a capable and caring man—is, with his wife Vi, still with us to this day as our assistant and supporter.)

The special feature to me in all this development was the construction of three bridges over sizeable streams on the site. For this I recruited an old man from the North West whom I will never forget. He was a real ancient, wearing a naval officer's type cap, frizzled and shrivelled up, small and stooped. But he was a miniature power house and a fountain of skill and knowledge. I took him to the first crossing site.

"Can you do it?" I asked.

"Give me ten men with axes, a one-inch auger, and a tractor when I ask for it," he replied.

With timber selected and cut from the bush around, he built a bridge that would carry ten tons or more. All the timbers were adzed, fitted and slotted together, and secured in place with wooden pegs he had shaped on site. A work of art and skill.

In short, within four years there was an active operation on the go. Four thousand head of cattle were settled in. These were grouped in herds of two- to three-hundred, enclosed in paddocks of around three thousand acres. Two paddocks were allocated to a herd; the cattle grazed each paddock for four months of the year and then moved to the one next to it. In this way, they grazed, or browsed, each area during the same season only for one period every two years, a simple form of rotation to allow different forms of plant life to recover.

This set-up was served by forty miles of roads and five cattle handling centres complete with holding pens, most of the construction work being done by hand labour. Boreholes for water

150

were sunk and cattle spray races erected at each handling centre. Five watering dams were constructed by heavy earth-moving equipment, and one hundred and twenty-five miles of steel fencing put up. Housing for resident workers and cattle men were completed, and a block of stores and offices built. The stage was reached when we were able to distribute home-bred young breeding heifers for stocking Government schemes elsewhere, destined to build up the herds for upcoming cattle farmers around the country.

Bernard's objective was achieved. The commercial cattle herd had been stabilised and was starting to grow again, and the local beef market secured. It was very fulfilling and satisfying.

Once a start had been made on all this, I drove the new Land Rover up to Hillwood to bring back Anne and Helen (the other children were in boarding school by this time). We travelled down with our light goods and Trudy our dog but minus our cat, which had escaped from its cage at the last minute and took to a roving life around the farm.

The residential holding in the corner of the property had been purchased and this became our home for the next four years, and the headquarters of the ranch. They were happy and fulfilling years, although we had to send the older children to South Africa to boarding school and cope with the stresses of that. Julia and Helen attended the Kitwe Primary School on our doorstep and did well there, a lovely young English lady teacher instilling in Helen a love for school, which proved invaluable. Julia had started school at Sakeji in the North West, but as soon as we were settled in we brought her to be at home, a good move for her at this time, and she did well in our new and happy environment.

The house was large with plenty of room to live, play and work with little managerial interference from above although much encouragement. We made a wonderful group of friends in the nearest town and often, especially over the weekends, were crowded with visitors for tennis or swimming or just to drink tea. We became part of a lively social world, and I gradually got back into the run of the farming community and wider activities after our time in the more remote North West. It was a time of action, achievement and fun, and we had a happy home there. All our holidays were spent making trips to South Africa, ferrying the children to or from school, or visiting them there. We had a Peugeot Station wagon that covered thousands of miles in those days, and which never let us down.

There are many people who featured in our lives and small incidents that occurred during those years, worthy of recall. One such person was Arthur, a young man from the U.K. who had come out under a British Service Overseas scheme. He was a tough, hard-working farm lad from the north of England, but temperamentally quite unsuited for working on his own in challenging situations. He had not reacted well to some of the challenges he was asked to face, and was in danger of being sent home, a disgrace he did not deserve. All he needed was a boss and some clear direction, and I was asked to take him on as a sort of salvage job, which I was glad to do. He came and lived in our home, worked very well with the men, and made a big hands-on contribution to the development work in many areas.

As I said, he needed an authority figure and he constantly referred to his farmer grandfather back in the U.K. who had obviously filled that role in his life. In coming to Zambia, he had been on the loose and had gone rather overboard. Now he called me "Boss" as he saw me in that role, seemed much more comfortable, and became a productive member of our team. But it was like riding a good and powerful yet unpredictable horse. I had to make it clear I was in charge, just once, which he accepted gladly.

His hobbies were playing rugby and the trumpet, and after a Saturday afternoon and evening at the local Rugby Club playing one (rugby), he would return home late in the evening and play the other (the trumpet) in the house. He knew only two tunes, *Rule Brittania* and *God Save the Queen*, which were not really appreciated by the family at midnight on a Saturday night.

Another incident comes to mind. We had been out one evening and on our return, were told by the Gateman that one of the horsemen was dying in his house. We had recruited a group of six horsemen from the Southern Province who were experienced in handling cattle. They were invaluable on their horses for the weekly mustering of each herd—a five-day-a-week activity—and were tough, independent and reliable. The sick man was one of them and we drove straight to his house, knowing that he was the last man to make a fuss about nothing.

I drew up to his house where a crowd had gathered. I waited outside while Anne quickly pushed her way in, assessed the situation in seconds and took active control. The next minute, a window was thrown open and an *mbwabula* (charcoal brazier) came hurling out, live coals scattering in all directions. Next, there was a hasty exit of folk through the door like a flushed group of startled hens, who had all crammed in to witness the expected demise of their comrade. These were followed by Anne who had initiated the exit, and then came the supposedly dying man supported by two others as they brought him into the fresh air. It was a simple case of carbon monoxide poisoning, caused by a charcoal brazier burning in an enclosed room with no escape from the noxious fumes, and any spare oxygen being used up by the sympathetic crowd. The simple remedy was fresh air. Sadly, this carbon monoxide poisoning is not an uncommon cause of death in Zambia.

The mention of these horsemen brings to mind that whole group of men. They were enthusiastic types who loved action, from a tiny youngster who rode a dappled mare that was inclined to buck, to Job, the senior horseman, who was an experienced tractor driver but preferred the rough and tumble of cattle work in wet dung and clouds of dust. George was one of them; a bearded, gentle giant of a man, he was simple and straight-forward and regularly rode the most difficult horse that kicked like a mule and was unrideable unless worked every day. George's smile was infectious even when asked to do the most difficult task. His love-hate relationship with that big, ungainly chestnut was interesting; he said it was the horse who found the cattle in the thick bush, not him. It never headed for home if given a free rein. I saw him one day on his own, driving a large herd of cows—over two hundred with their calves—along the road towards the pens of Number One unit. The cattle were all under control as he walked along behind them, carefully carrying his big hat full of early mushrooms. The big chestnut was quietly following close behind him of its own accord.

We had very good relations with our huge team of workers. Discipline was necessary of course, but apart from a few rascals who tried their luck, our care of and interest in them was rewarded by loyalty and honesty.

The development of the property only just kept ahead of the incoming consignments of cattle. I would get a phone call in the evening from the buyer, a Scotsman called Murray.

"We've railed a consignment of two hundred heifers. They should be with you tomorrow afternoon."

The problem was that the railway siding was in the industrial area of the Copperbelt town of Kitwe, with no off-loading facilities or holding pens for livestock. The railway trucks were simply backed alongside a raised embankment, level with the truck doors, and until the doors were opened and the animals poured out we had no idea what to expect. My team became expert at handling whatever did emerge as the truck doors were opened, which was usually a rush of bewildered, excited, angry, and often wild cattle.

We would calm them down by just quietly surrounding them and keeping them there near the trucks for a while, talking and letting them get used to us, and then we would move them off. The next challenge was that the off-loading usually coincided with Kitwe's rush hour at five o'clock, which meant busy traffic. Moving a big mob of cattle that had previously known only wide-open bush paddocks, herding them along busy streets and roads through heavy and impatient traffic, was no joke. But we never lost a single one. They would all arrive safely at the ranch to be kraaled overnight before being checked the next day and assigned to the peace of their own bush paddocks to graze.

One other incident I must mention. Right at the heart of the property, we were experiencing continual bush fires. We couldn't find the source so one day I went with a group of the guys who were as fed up with this as I was, to see what we could find. Ranging through the bush we eventually found the trouble. It was an old man who had made his camp between two huge ant-hills—a shelter of grass, a rough bed, his fire and his dogs—and who was literally living off the land. There was little food, although there was evidence of how he lived. He was trapping small animals, eating seasonal fruit along with fish from the streams, and living a simple life of solitude in a complete absence of stress. I almost envied him. It was sad to disturb him, but there was no alternative. He understood the inevitable, quietly packed his few belongs, his bow and arrows, spear and traps, shouldered them and moved away followed by his dogs, to find a home elsewhere.

The men told me this was nothing unusual: old men deciding communal life was not that attractive and leaving to make a solitary life of their own, although areas in which they could live like this were getting scarce. They told me they had once found a similar camp with an old man lying dead on his bed, a lonely ending. The following annual bush fire would probably have wiped it all away.

As I said, these were happy years. I had a splendid gang of workers, things were becoming well organised, the cattle were settled in and doing well, and I had a free hand in running things within the overall Company policy.

However, there was one drawback to all this. Although there seemed to be endless funds for development of these ranches positioned in every Province, for some reason best known to themselves, the powers now in place adopted a policy of economising on management. Bernard and his team were gone, as well as the World Bank General Manager appointee from Kenya. They were replaced with men, good in themselves, but with no understanding of what made an effective operation like ours tick.

At a management meeting with the bosses, we were told that farm managers were plentiful on the world market (probably right technically speaking) and there was no chance of Managers' terms of employment being anything other than what they currently were. We could do what we liked; we could easily be replaced. With a family of five children to care for and educate, Anne and I were living hand-to-mouth, with nothing to spare for emergencies or the future. With the greatest regret, we had to look further afield.

Within a year, most of the original State Ranch managers had gone. I will not comment on those who replaced them. The rot had set in and it was the beginning of a rapid downward spiral and the ending of what had been an inspired project, one which had saved the productive part of the national cattle herd. A tragedy. All the work, not only on our operation but on all the others as well, and all that funding, was allowed to go down the drain. Within a year of my leaving, ten percent of the cattle on our ranch were missing and unaccounted for, so the external Auditor told me. Within ten years, the property had been abandoned, the development vandalised, and the place covered with squatters and illicit charcoal burners. All that effort for nothing.

For ourselves, we did not wait for this to happen. Family needs had to be met and we had to meet them. I was offered a job by our Head Office as a sort of senior roving Ranch Manager, travelling around the now under-managed ranches all over the country and propping up the now largely inadequate management. I certainly did not fall for that one. We had to make a move, once again. A new manager was appointed in my place; I wound up the business side of things, wrote and handed him detailed hand-over notes. These I found in a rubbish pit the very next day, a clear indication of what was to come.

13

IT WAS A LONG ROAD

"Strangers and pilgrims on the earth."

Hebrews 11:13

Before we had time to get really depressed about all this another possibility suddenly presented itself, quite unexpectedly. It was with one of the great mining corporations, who to my surprise approached me with the offer to manage a group of their small farms on the Copperbelt. This I accepted; it was a quick and ready answer to our needs of a home and employment in an environment I knew well. Their terms and conditions were very attractive and met the educational needs for the children, and we could not afford a gap. Unfortunately, within a year, this venture led into a rapid and not very well-planned agricultural expansion, which fell flat on its face within four years.

I do not wish to dwell on this rather unhappy period of our family life that took us from one of the mining towns, Chililabombwe, to the capital Lusaka and the commercial farming area of Chisamba. We moved house about four times. Our social group changed into one in which we were not entirely comfortable, and which was not the best for our now teenage children. However, we did make a few good friends who have stood the test of time, but it brought pressures on our family life which we could have done without.

In the work area I learned a great deal more. I learned about people in the business and work world on a wider scale than had ever come my way before. I met a few great men, men of power and of the highest moral and business standards, especially one man who must remain nameless but who headed one of the largest and most powerful mining groups in Southern Africa. He was a humble and uncomplicated person with a clear mind and a penetrating approach, all of which he used with discretion and wisdom. The brief encounter I enjoyed with him on just one occasion when he visited the farms is etched clearly in my mind.

But there were others—very wealthy men who sat on distant Boards as Company Directors—who were ruthless; their money was their power, and this they used to the full. I learned what it was to be stabbed in the back by men I had trusted. I came across those who were trying to build their own little empires, or just their reputations and positions in this vast, overall set-up. I saw vicious men who would sacrifice others to protect their own short-comings. And I saw how not to build what could have been a profitable enterprise on false or loaded information and manipulated financial figures to make things look good.

I saw the foolishness of placing incompetent people in positions of power to please others or because of who they were on the social scale. I also experienced the frustration of decisions being made in distant offices that stifled the management on the ground. In this situation I battled for nearly four years. I was in charge of all livestock in the organisation, and as such bore the responsibility of setbacks (of which there were many under pressure from above), without having the authority or right means in my hand to prevent them. When any successes did come, there was a line of those wanting to take the credit.

Priorities were upside down; business lunches, evening events and unnecessary meetings came before the daily work on the farms and grassroots control. The trappings of the set-up overshadowed the basic problems and needs. Eventually, a cover-up over the dubious purchase and consignment of a group of bulls that had its roots at the very heart of this great organisation, became evident to me and I brought it to light. If it had not been exposed, my department would have had to bear the consequences. I would not face that. But I was finished from then on and it was made very evident.

I was paid well, but they wanted to own me. I was told my family took far too much priority in my time and thinking. It seemed to me the view was that money could buy anything, even superseding family life and responsibility. I could have all I asked for in funding and support at that level, but the Company had to come first. I had to think that through and make a decision.

Perhaps it was this that brought about a period of health problems, and I ended up in hospital following an operation, minus an appendix and gall stones but with the same complication that had caused my father's death. It was a near thing. I had mentioned this medical history to the surgeon previously, and they were prepared. I owe my life to a lovely little West Indian nurse who responded with speed to my call for help but it took me a while to pull out of this. In my absence, others had taken control of my responsibilities, and it was obvious when I returned that no longer did I fit.

I also learned that what goes around comes around, and there is a day of reckoning. In this particular apple, there was not only a worm but the fruit itself was hollow. Serious and able guardians of the multi-millions controlled by this great organisation smelled a rat, followed their noses, and penetrated the superficial peel, finding both the hollow and the worm. Millions had been lost and heads rolled, sadly including some of those who had seen what was happening and its inevitable outcome, but had been powerless to prevent it. Another project with great potential had gone down the drain. I heard years later that those who had truly been the cause of the downfall of what under right management could have been a great success, had met their own demise.

I had now experienced first-hand, in two quite different projects and situations, that too much money is almost worse than too little, and that the priceless key to every successful project is experienced and capable on-the-ground management. As I lay in hospital recuperating, I decided I had had enough. I was not going to spend my best working years, backed by hard-earned experience, in building something up only to see it destroyed and come to nothing. From now on I would paddle my own canoe.

Strangely this was not yet to be. While in hospital, I was approached with a proposition to join Anne's uncle, a much-respected surgeon. He had over the years put together a large grazing property on the Copperbelt and a breeding herd of cattle, with some infrastructure. He very much wanted this to reach its full potential, and was aware that in order for it to do so, direct management input was needed. He was retiring, and his family at that time were not interested in the property other than as a pleasant family home, which it was. Was I interested?

We talked it over, and it seemed that here was not only a home and situation where we could be comfortable among our extended family, but also an immediate project into which I could throw myself and that held long term prospects. Terms were discussed, decisions made, and as participants in this family Company with farm and business management responsibility, we were once more on our way.

We were there for seven years, and I dare to say that things prospered. The economic situation at that time favoured farming in general. The country and its leaders had settled into the new mode of running their own affairs, and matters were generally moving along comfortably. We took advantage of prevailing conditions; new quick-turnover projects were introduced and expanded if they succeeded, or discarded if they showed no promise. The cattle herd was increased to the full potential of the property, pastures were improved, and the trading turnover of the operation doubled itself each year, showing a satisfactory profit. The basic infrastructure that had previously been developed was good; it just needed maintenance, strengthening, and building upon.

I enjoyed the pleasure of a good relationship with Anne's uncle, and an increasing respect for him in every way. He had the remarkable combination of a scientific mind and a practical down-to-earth approach, and I learned much from him as we discussed practical daily problems together. He gave me some very useful guidelines, while supporting my management in every way. He had a wonderful sense of humour too, which always helps.

When I arrived on this farm there were a few—six, I seem to remember—pedigree Sussex cows; two had been part of a larger importation from the U.K. to Zambia. Pedigree Sussex bulls had been widely used on the main herd, so from that source and in upgrading selected animals from their progeny, we set about establishing a larger, registered purebred herd. We imported a further six pedigree heifers and a bull from the U.K., and a bull from South Africa. I had the pleasure and benefit of visiting breeders in those countries on their home ground, and learned much in meeting with them and selecting animals. Soon we had home-bred bulls that were surplus to our requirements and we entered into the Showing and Bull Sale business.

While I thoroughly enjoyed the detailed work of building this part of our operation and all it entailed it also proved profitable for the farm, not only in cash returns but by using home-bred bulls to improve the quality of the main breeding herd and the beef animals we produced. We had no difficulty in finding a market, both for slaughter animals and for breeding stock. It also introduced me to the wider world of this industry in South Africa and the U.K., where I came to know personalities with considerable experience in the breed as well as the wide range of stock and pool of genetics out there.

During that time, I was appointed chairman of the Zambia Herd Book Society, and served in that capacity for three or four years. Council meetings and Society matters, Shows and Sales became an increasing part of my life. Under the Herd Book Society there were ten different breeds registered; foundation stock was being imported from South Africa and Europe, and regular Council meetings kept the ball rolling. Chairing a Council consisting of ten strong personalities who were each in turn Chairman of their own Breed Committees was a challenge; these were people who certainly could not be pushed around.

While on this farm, we built a happy home life with many friends. Our income was adequate for our needs and those of our children, now growing up. Many gatherings took place in our lovely home situated on the banks of the Kafue River, and our first family wedding took place here when Liz married her English husband, Geoff. Work was fulfilling but not overwhelming; we had time for holidays, mostly taken up with school trips or meeting up with the family on their school holidays in South Africa or Zimbabwe.

Living by a large river was fun, as it provided a continual and varied flowing stream, sometimes flood level, other times low, not only of water with its flotsam and jetsam, but of varied wildlife, from hippo and crocs to birdlife. Pets had always played a big part in our family life, and it was here I had the finest dog I have ever owned, a huge Alsatian called King who was faithful to a fault. During my absences, he guarded Anne and the family without let-up. To the best of my knowledge, he only ever bit one person—the same one—twice, and that was because he came up behind me without warning. King had the unnerving habit of staring without blinking and in complete silence at anyone of whom he was suspicious, without making a move but ready for instant action. Helen's miniature daschund, Heidi, was his devoted and very vocal back-up.

At the end of this period, and with great regret, the time came when we had to relinquish our home, all we had built here, our hoped-for prospects, and the good relations that had been established. Success has its pitfalls, and we had by now learned that nothing is static. The immediate family, who held the major interest in this private company, began to take an interest in this now profitable enterprise. Whereas before they had enjoyed it as a pleasant home setting, they now saw an operation with a sustainable and profitable future. Once more, as with Hillwood, there was not room for us all, and as minor shareholders Anne and I could only give way. It could have been tricky, and there were some difficult moments. However, we managed to come to acceptable terms of disengagement, and taking out our interest in the company in the form of cattle, we moved once more.

We were leaving behind a viable business, given the right management. I had that satisfaction, whatever its future might be, knowing that the initial purpose had been achieved. This time, this move, please God, would be for the last time. We were now fifty years old, but we still had the energy and ability to pack up once more, and we did. Like Abraham of old, we seemed to have no continuing city, and we had no idea of what God had in store for us in our immediate future.

We were in for more surprises.

14

WHERE DO WE GO FROM HERE?

"Go in peace."

1 Samuel 20:42

It is not uncommon, I have noted, for folk in their middle years to reach a specific life crisis, sometimes termed a "mid-life crisis", which has to be faced up to and dealt with. The important thing is just how they deal with it. Whatever the crisis may be, and there are dozens of options, the point is that it is not the end or the beginning of the end. At least it need not be. And it certainly should not be used as an excuse to go out of control or do stupid things.

It is no lie that today is the first day of the rest of our lives. We just have to stay steady under fire. The challenge for Anne and me was to face and handle positively whatever confronted us in the full realisation that it was only mid-life, not end-life, and there could well be many effective and productive years still to come. For us, the question we had faced a few times before was there once more: where do we go from here?

The question applied not only to location but also to our mindset and whole approach to life. We could just retreat, creep into a hole and feel hard done-by and defeated, or adopt a negative approach and stagnate for the years to come. Or, we could take the attitude that this was how things are but the world was still out there, and there must be a place for us where we could live out effective lives and make a contribution to the whole! This was, after all, the beginning of the rest of our lives, however long or short they might turn out to be.

So, we took stock and looked realistically at where we were. Our family had grown up now. Liz and Brian were both married, Sheila and Julia were also launched out in life, and Helen was in her last year of school. While our home was still theirs in every sense, in part we were on our own. We put the negatives behind us, and concentrated on the positives.

As a part of the farming world, we felt sure we had a place; we were known and hopefully appreciated. We had a living asset in the form of cattle for which we needed to find a home. In the course of the last ten years, and especially in the cattle breeding world, we had acquired good friends. Invaluable. And we had health and energy. All we needed was the will to maintain faith, assess the situation, and look carefully at our options. Sure enough, as we dug deeper they were there.

I was determined that from now on I would paddle my own canoe and build an independent venture for the benefit and security of just our own family. Not selfish really, but we were shattered to see ventures into which we had put so much of our personal time and energy, as well as loyalty and expertise, now lying in ruins. Putting ourselves into the hands of our God, we began to explore.

Circumstances and friendships led us to look carefully at the commercial farming area of Mkushi in the Central Province of Zambia, where there were a number of vacant or available farms. We looked at several of these, and ended up with three or four possibilities. Multiple opportunities can be confusing, but it always surprises me that if we stand back, wait patiently and look objectively at our options with an open mind, things sort themselves out on their own; the non-starters become evident and the right choices slot into place, which is exactly what happened at this juncture of our lives. I can only and do attribute this to the guiding hand of God whom we have always tried to honour.

At a closer look, two options clearly struck themselves off the list as non-starters. One of these farms I could have bought for the value of the small herd of cattle on it and that was about what it was worth. Another apparently attractive possibility was knocked out for us by a counter offer from a third party, which we certainly could not match by a long way. The seller kindly and openly told me of this, knowing that it would rule me out, and we could only congratulate him. We were pleased for him; his wife had health problems and he could now relocate to be with her full time.

Unless we looked further afield, there was just one remaining option. While having some limitations, it ticked the boxes of the immediate needs for relocating our hundred-plus herd of breeding cows, while providing us with a home as well as strong and gracious moral support and encouragement from a family who made the farm available to us, and who in time became our intimate and valued friends.

Thus, in May and June 1980, we re-located ourselves, our dogs, our furniture, fittings, and few belongings to Kapanda Farm, Mkushi, and this has been our family home and base for the last 36 years. Perhaps it is appropriate to say at this point that we have never regretted this move, or considered at any time or for any reason a move to another place or country. It has been a happy home for us both, and for any and all of our family when they come to see us. Just about all of them have done so over the years, but I do not want to jump that gun.

As we moved into this new situation, we first had to take stock of our assets. For a start, our ready cash was hardly worth a mention, and what we had was mostly eaten up in buying a one-ton single cab Pick-up truck, a reliable means of transport being essential. The breeding cows were due to give us a calf crop within six months; while being of good value as book assets they were not exactly ready cash. We had a farm that had some basic infrastructure but which required input to become productive. We had a large house that had been empty for eleven years; while it had been kept operative on a maintenance level, it needed repairs and upgrading. I approached the Banks for support.

The first interview I had was with a senior manager of one of the largest U.K. Banks that had branches in many parts of the world. The interview in his office lasted about ten minutes. I started by telling him frankly of my situation and what I was looking for. He asked me what the long term thrust of my new venture would be, and I told him cattle. The cattle I had were my major asset and my primary interest and field of experience. He said the Bank would certainly not be interested in that; cattle were poor business, he said, and an even poorer basis on which to secure Bank support. He recommended crops. I was astounded.

I had by now been in the cattle industry in the country for over thirty years, and from my own experience and observation of others, I knew well that he was wrong. For a start, cattle not only grow physically but they multiply as well. Not even gold does that; a bar of gold remains a bar of gold, unchanged for a hundred years. There was more to it than that. If a cattle herd is managed properly and with vision, the very quality and therefore the overall value of the herd can be increased. I knew of no better investment, and still don't. They have always been the core of our business and they have never let us down, and have rewarded every right decision. But one must be patient.

In growing crops, I knew you could, and I repeat *could*, make good money. But they were short term, needed the right farm and soils, and required big capital inputs in the way of machinery, which I did not have. What I did have was a herd of good cows that I well knew were my ready-made foundation.

As I said, the interview did not last ten minutes; we were talking a different language and no ways did I want to be indebted to a Bank with that short-sighted outlook. I thanked him, said I would think about it (I had already thought) and left. Incidentally, time would have shown that Bank Manager which of his farming clients survived the difficult years of the eighties, but he was by then long-gone to higher things in his profession.

I went to see the next Bank in line. I had had some experience with them in our previous situation. Thankfully, they were prepared to listen to common sense, and I was to enjoy their support for many years. They came to see me on the farm, a wise move on their part as they could see first-hand what I was talking about, and meet us on our home ground. After a drive around the farm we sat in our sitting room, worked out a business plan and cash flow, modest and realistic, and they left. A few days later we received a letter of offer, and we were on our way.

I do remember saying to the manager I dealt with, "I am making a commitment to you by signing these papers. Are you by the same token making a commitment to me? You are obviously prepared to trust me, but I must always and in all circumstances, be able to trust you. Bounce one of my cheques for whatever reason and I will cease to be your client." I remember too quoting this old saying, "In for a penny, in for a pound" as our approach to the venture. I told him I would make it a rule that I would never accumulate debts; our policy would be to pay cash or have short term credit accounts, and they, the Bank, would be my only creditor. Years later, I was told this was a deciding point for the Bank in supporting us.

If my thoughts on dealing with Banks are of any value, I have always been absolutely open in my dealings with them. If times are tough, I tell them. If deadlines can't be met for whatever reason, I tell them. But, and this I learned from my Dad, never, ever allow the Bank to control you, or to have a greater investment in your business than you have. In fact, I made it an aim never to expose myself to the Bank for more than twenty-five per cent of the value of my liquid assets. It was close to the bone at times, but we made it. I also once advised my son Brian, "Use the Bank's available support, but never let them control you." We did not become the biggest farmers in the area, but we were secure.

That was the first step, an important one without which we would have been very restricted. Now we had the resources to work with, we had to get going on the ground. Our cattle were settled, and our good neighbour from whom we had acquired this farm allowed us to use his cattle dip for the weekly dipping. Fences had to be strengthened, access roads made, security set up, workers to be employed and land cleared of trees and re-growth so we could plant some crops; in addition, our own cattle dip and working kraals had to be built. It took time but drawing on past experience, I was able to get this all going without delay.

Our house, however, was a bit of a challenge. When Anne first saw it she was shocked, in fact she even shed a tear or two, as it was very different from our neat and lovely home of seven years on the Kafue River. The garden had been huge at one time under the previous owners, but was now overgrown. There was no view as the prolific Pride of India trees had surrounded the house. Inside was the old furniture, which we gradually moved out to give place to our own.

It was a big house comprising four double bedrooms, a large sitting room with rather small windows, and a spacious back kitchen area. It was evident that even the original finishing touches had been limited.

The immediate problem were the bats and rats who had established the right of residence. As we sat in the sitting room of an evening we could see rats running up and down the pillars on the veranda to sample the leftovers of the dogs' food. We acquired a couple of half-grown cats and the rats soon got the message, and from then on just paid passing visits. Bats were more persistent and around the house, where the walls met the roof, their entry points had to be blocked. But sometimes, they still managed to squeeze through. Helen's teenage screams called me into her bedroom one night to remove a bat that had crawled into bed with her.

The water system was a bit primitive and tadpoles would flow through the cold tap and into the bath. Helen used the kitchen vegetable sieve held under the tap to strain them out and throw them into a bucket. Occasionally a mudfish would block the supply pipe, cutting off the water flow completely.

With the help of a good carpenter, a bricklayer, and eventually a painter, we soon made the house homely and to our liking. Thirty-seven years later we are still making improvements or doing re-construction which, had unlimited funds been available, we could have done at the start. But we have come to love and be comfortable in our home, and have enjoyed the company of so many family and friends visiting us here over the years. The garden was also coaxed into shape, although we reduced its size considerably and surrounded it with a security fence; whilst not being that secure it at least outlined our home area defended by our various dogs, and kept roaming cattle, sheep, and unwanted dogs or jackals outside.

I was not an experienced crop farmer, and growing even a small area of maize and soya beans was not a success. It was small-scale but soil fertility and structure needed to be improved, and machinery had to be hired or borrowed. I eventually received a contract to grow a good acreage of seed maize; this was mainly hand work and we did well from that. However, I had to look at more intensive cultivation of high value crops on a small area. Land was limited and the cattle herd was growing fast. Consequently, we installed drip irrigation and for many years grew six hectares of tomatoes annually. These did well and helped us build up our cattle herd to significant proportions and value.

The registered pedigree herd of Sussex cattle became my lucrative hobby, with Shows and Bull Sales being a part of that. I then launched out and bought a small group of registered Boran cows. These were an indigenous breed imported from Kenya and which became and still are a very important part of the industry. With these two groups I could and did breed all our own bull needs, the sale of surplus bulls paying the costs.

The Boran venture built up, and after about ten years I was able to sell the increased herd to a friend who wanted to get into the breed. It had been a very profitable venture with a clear-cut input, maintenance, output, and final sale operation. The bulls produced and sold during those years more than paid for any upkeep and investments we had made, while the heifers were kept to increase the number and quality of the breeding cow herd. All very satisfactory; but they had to go. I found that I was spreading myself too thinly in the different sections of the farm, which were clashing as they competed for time and attention, and I had to downsize a bit.

When we first started at Kapanda, I had bought a couple of Jersey cows to provide us with our own milk. As I was already using artificial insemination to maintain and expand the genetic breadth of the Sussex herd, I started using the best available Jersey bull semen from America on our Jersey cows. In no time, the dairy herd of these hardy little cattle began to expand, as did the milk sales. As I did all the inseminations myself, the need for which could come at any time, I had to be available as much as possible. And, though I say it myself, I became quite skilled at this tricky technique as the statistics showed: they were equal to those of the British Milk Marketing Board Inseminators. But, and I must add this, when studying an English agricultural correspondence course years earlier, I had learned that when breeding cattle, the aim must always be to improve quality as well as increase numbers. This I have done all my years as much as I could, and have never regretted it. Thus, throughout our working years at Kapanda, using my acquired skills to put into practice what I had learned so long ago, quality Jersey and Sussex cattle genes were not only introduced but established on the farm.

On Kapanda Farm, we held our own and made steady progress. Every year was a learning curve, but I ask, when do we ever stop learning? Our community life also built up, and we made many good friends. We joined the Country Club, attended functions, helped where we could, and while giving out when it was called for we were so often on the receiving end. It is a happy community of farming folk, and although there are tensions here and there they never overshadow the communal life.

In our early years here, it was a mixed community. While many farmers were from much the same origin as ourselves, there was a body of Greek farmers too who had been expelled from Tanzania and made their homes here as skilled tobacco growers. There were a couple of families from what was then Yugoslavia, and a Swedish national who had originated from Czechoslovakia. Some of the oldies had seen service in WW2, and it was good to see second generation youngsters beginning to come home, some with their South African wives, and take over as their fathers stepped down. This changed rather over the years, but I will leave that for now.

Suffice to say it was an extraordinarily supportive community, and mutual help often went well beyond the normal; when asked for it was given without restraint. This we experienced one night when we were woken by a neighbouring friend (who farmed about half an hour's drive from us) at our bedroom window, near tears and asking for our help. His wife was very ill; he had carried her onto our veranda and laid her on a chair. With great good fortune, we had a Swedish friend staying with us who was a nurse, and after one quick check she said, "Where is the nearest hospital?" Two hours away. Neither our vehicle nor theirs was suitable for the long trip. I quickly jumped in our truck and dashed across to our closest neighbour, just ten minutes down the road, blowing my horn as I turned into his drive. He was out with his torch in his shorty pyjamas by the time I had pulled up.

"Quick, David, your Range Rover. A hospital case. Y is very ill at our house."

Without a moment's hesitation on his part, we threw the tools and other things out of his vehicle, lowered the back seats, put in a mattress, fuelled up, and away he went without a second thought. That was how it was. And we were privileged to become an accepted part of it all.

But there was more to come.

15

THE LONG ROAD, AND
WHERE IT LED

"I being in the way, the Lord led me."

Genesis 24:27

It sometimes surprises us when we stop to think about it, that Anne and I have spent more than half our adult life at Kapanda Farm. The years have gone by so quickly, and so much has happened during this time. As family people, we have graduated from being parents to grandparents and then great-grandparents. Only our granddaughter, Nikki, her husband, Alex, and their three children are still living in Zambia, and wonderfully are here on the farm with us. Or more accurately, we are here with them. Sheila and her family, Bonnie, and their two boys, Sean and Peter, are nearby in South Africa. The rest, all twenty of them, are scattered around the world in Australia, Israel, Germany and the U.K.

Most of them, though, still regard Zambia, and particularly Mkushi, as their roots and even home to which they can come back any time to stay and visit with us. And they do. Some of them, especially those who grew up here, miss it terribly and long to come back, even just to enjoy the African atmosphere and the feeling of welcome and home, the smells and the space, the dry and the wet, the people and the warm welcome they always receive. Once all that is in your blood, they say, you never lose it. Very true. But of course, they have their own careers, work and lives to build, wherever those may call them.

In recounting one's own experiences and path in life, in other words one's story, it is not possible to ignore the wider world in which we lived, and still do, the things that went on around us, and how we were and are affected by them. The country in which we live might be a very large one geographically, set in an even more spread out region known broadly as Southern Africa, yet it really is quite small. By this I mean that what happens in countries around us have a very significant impact on us. Cross-communication and travel were always a part of life here in general, and we were continually aware of situations a thousand and two thousand miles away, say in Harare or Johannesburg; more so perhaps than people in London are aware of situations or of what people's thoughts and their reactions might be in, say, Manchester or Carlisle, let alone Scotland, a mere few hundred easy miles away.

Thus, the political unrest and fighting in the Congo and Angola, the very bitter civil war in Rhodesia-Zimbabwe, and the political upheaval and changes in South Africa all affected us profoundly through the years. As countries and as individuals, we were so inter-dependent economically, socially, and politically. Part of the reason for this was that the boundaries established by colonial powers over a hundred years ago, while following water ways and catchment areas, cut right across some tribal and economically interdependent communities. This meant that unrest in one country could affect at least some of the peoples with whom there were close ties in another country. This was the case not only for the African peoples and tribes, but also for expatriate populations from the western and eastern parts of the world, either those families and communities with a long history in Africa or those who had come to stay more recently. They all had cross-border ties and relationships.

The waves of social unrest, inter-sectional fighting, crop failures, economic instability or failure, health factors, political crises and changes, wherever they might be, all had an unsettling effect to the very perimeters of our region. The clearest example of this was the Rhodesian war and its after effects, which reached into our very rural neighbourhoods and caused great tension. Relationships *between* the white and black communities were affected, as well as *within* each separate community. It created suspicion, ill-informed opinions and reactions, all of which had a negative effect.

Rumours abounded, but events and specific actions were also a part. To name but a few: a couple who were connected to our extended family were murdered in their own farm home one Sunday night, this allegedly by agents of the South African National Congress whom they had unknowingly offended. In other instances, Rhodesian forces flew into Zambia by helicopter and destroyed road and rail bridges right in our own district. The wife of one of our local farmers was astounded to be stopped by a white soldier on a bridge one morning when on her way to town.

"Good morning madam," he said. "We shall be blowing up the bridge in five minutes. Which side would you like to be?"

The husband of a school friend of one of our daughters from years before, took part in a long-distance, armed raid from the then Rhodesia, penetrating as far as Lusaka. And one day, our hospitality to a very disorganised group of young South Africans in a rather doubtful Land Rover for one night brought us under suspicion, as they were later caught and arrested as spies.

In a wider sense, our dependence on South Africa for agricultural, mining and transport inputs was in jeopardy as these were severely restricted at times. The country's fuel supply was cut off due to trouble to the south of us, and it had to be road-hauled from East Africa along what was known as the Hell Run. Anyone with a lorry could take part, register, pick up empty drums from the oil depots and go. It must have cost the Government a fortune, and one truck in five had an accident. One young farmer I knew who had inherited his father's farm along with his substantial debts, repaired their old farm truck and steadily drove up and down, to and from Dar Es Salaam, until he had paid off all the debts.

Thousands of fighters of one of Rhodesia's rival political groups were camped in Zambia; private aircraft were mostly grounded, and things were very tense at times. It was wise to tread carefully, not to take sides or even discuss things of which we knew little. There were nasty incidents in towns that are best forgotten, and it was often hard to understand all that was going on. The wise thing was to mind one's own business, keep one's head down and mouth shut, and hope and pray that what was a confusing and unhappy situation would eventually sort itself out. And it did. By the grace of God, we steered our way through it all and emerged intact and on track. Massive changes had taken place in the process, however, and to these we adjusted ourselves, and to any new situations as they came about.

Perhaps our main contribution over this time that spanned some years was to try and maintain stability and continuity in our own particular spheres. I cannot measure this, or attempt to assess what our personal or community efforts might have achieved in this respect. Enough to say that with some exceptions our own community remained stable, produced much needed food, and provided employment for workers dependent on us. We had to adjust, both in our mind sets as well as our modes of operation, quite drastically in some cases, and could not always look south for things like health support and education.

When things became really difficult in Rhodesia (which later became Zimbabwe), we had to extract Helen from her school in Salisbury (now Harare) where she was so happy and doing well, and send her to England to complete her education. The cost and effort strained all our resources at the time. For a start, the urgent need to get her home from Harare almost reached crisis level. At very long range, I arranged for her to fly from Harare to Victoria Falls. To retrieve her from there, I drove to Livingstone, up along the Zambezi River and across the border on the pontoon into Botswana, then back along a dirt road following the Zambezi

River down and into Rhodesia. There I picked her up at the little airport where the local air flight landed, an hour or two late, then back the way I came to Livingstone, followed by the long drive home. A three-day expedition with many police control points along the way, as they were on high alert.

In some ways, our lines of communication shortened or were just cut off; in others, they became very extended. The secret was to keep our heads, adjust to changes or frustrations, and get on with it. Or alternatively, to get out, which some did during those years. Hindsight is easy, but I am glad that we made the decision to stay put. Through all those years many did not and relocated elsewhere. Some did so with success and established themselves and their families happily elsewhere. Many did not, even moving down several notches in their employment and income status. Previously owners, employers and producers on a considerable scale, they became second level employees in jobs well below their capacities. Others in the older age brackets just sat and grieved for the years that had gone by and the homes they had left. One person said to me after some years of contract work developing a farm for an agency, "The years I had in Africa were the most fulfilling time of my life." Many others who had spent the best part of their lives here felt the same, and regretted leaving it.

In writing all this, I am drawing on happenings which covered a time-span of probably fifty years. I was a participant in some small ways perhaps, but far more an observer. As an affected participant, I did have a close look at relocating the family to the U.K., and failing that then New Zealand or Australia. However, events and perhaps common sense eliminated these options.

It is a fact that there were difficulties for those who had expatriate roots. For the cynical they could be termed racial, and perhaps in some cases they were. However, I think they were far more genuinely cultural, and in some cases political. There were undoubtedly cultural barriers that were difficult to cross; there were ways of doing things or reasons for doing them that were different among the groups of people who came from different backgrounds and cultural roots. And I emphasise different, just *different*, not right or wrong. After all we, the expatriates, or non-African by race if not in our spirits and outlook, were in the minority. Some expats tried to be "African", a facade which the real Africans with their in-born discernment quickly saw through. Others became involved in or interfered with politics, often to their cost as they misjudged situations or failed to understand the aspirations of those they linked up with, and got caught in the crossfire.

For us, and I criticise no one else in this, we made the decision to be open to the fact of who we were. We had British passports and British we were. We identified with the changing circumstances, even though we did not initially perhaps like some of them. We respected the rules, even the new ones which we did not always appreciate. If we wanted to live in this new Rome (and we did), while maybe not always doing as Rome did we did as Rome required. We were given the status of card-carrying residents and as we accepted and respected the new regime so our fellow residents who were also citizens of their new country, appreciated and respected us. The important thing I believe in situations like this is to recognise and respect the views and standpoints of one another, and the interesting outcome has been a blending of ideas and thought patterns that has been beneficial to all.

As our old foreman Joseph said to me on more than one occasion when we differed in trying to reach a conclusion while resolving a problem, "You think about it like this, but we think about it like that," and between us we would reach an understanding. Perhaps he had come to understand my thought process as much as I bluffed myself I understood his. Anyway, especially in cases involving workers and their families or Government Officialdom, I just asked him outright, "What should we do?" until eventually he had the confidence and wisdom to say, "Boss, just leave it to me."

It is of interest to recall some of the incidents of these times. It was in the very early sixties that things fell apart in the Congo. The North Western and Copperbelt Provinces were right alongside the Border, and contacts had been close, continuous, and sometimes casual. The latter especially for those with bicycles and on foot and to whom officialdom was irrelevant as they moved to and fro visiting friends and relatives, and even casually trading. Unofficial roads and paths were everywhere as needed, and worn by constant use.

The Congo had been given Self Government and "Freedom" by Belgium in what seemed a hasty way, and with little preparation. It was a vast country with many different tribes who were, to say the least, not always on friendly terms with one another. It also had a very well-trained army previously commanded by the Belgians, which had great expectations and when these did not materialise in their "Freedom", they helped themselves. Mutiny by armed and organised forces is not funny, but did the remaining Belgians panic—oh my! From the Katanga Province, the beautiful town of Elisabethville, and the prosperous mines like Kolwezi and Jadoville, they just grabbed essentials like blankets and food and headed for the border along every available road and track. Their cars emerged from the bush in the most unlikely places onto the main road that passed near the border and lead up to the North West. It all seemed to happen overnight.

We were in Chingola at that time, although we had already moved house to Hillwood, and awoke one morning to this congestion and chaos. Traffic streamed south; a hasty border control was set up outside Chingola, and the line of vehicles stretched back five miles and more. Immigration officials were overwhelmed; none seemed able to speak French, and at first their main support was an Irish engineering contractor from the Mine who was fluent in the language. Then an English missionary lady who had been raised in the Congo appeared and joined the fray, managing to bring some order and authority to things. Just as well, as the Irishman who had been keeping up his strength over the many hours with a bottle of whisky, had finally buckled and was sleeping it off on the side of the road, having said a few uncalled-for words about the refugees before being overcome. The residents of Chingola rose to the occasion and carried out food, soup and drinks to the exhausted fugitives waiting their turn. The local post office was flooded with excited and confused folk trying to send telegrams in French and pay for them with Belgian Francs.

The fleeing people varied in their reactions to the unfortunate situation. Some were in sheer panic; others had suffered bad experiences and were in shock; and others still were just dully wanting to escape and get somewhere safe and secure. There were families with children and defensive mothers in control, while fathers defeatedly did what they were told; there were car-loads of men who took advantage of every opportunity and were uncaring of others, while others were polite and grateful to be safe. Most people did not know what to do or where they would go from there, but others were well organised and in control of themselves.

One person I remember so well, even fifty-six years later, was a stunningly attractive young blonde lady driving a new but very dusty Mercedes Benz, with the most beautiful, sun-bronzed baby boy asleep on the back seat of her well-ordered car. She was almost serene, and well in control of herself and her situation as she calmly waited her turn to be cleared through customs in the surrounding dust and heat. She was certainly out of character among the general panic. I wondered who she was, and who and where her husband was.

That day, I saw a great variety of people, from selfish to serving, from fearful to brave. Among these last was Howard, the Australian husband of Elizabeth, the French-speaking missionary lady whom I mentioned earlier, who heard of two ladies who had been stranded in some remote place and drove back against the exiting tide of vehicles to find them and bring them out. This was a dangerous thing to do at that time as excitement was high all round, and out-of-control soldiers were firing at random at vehicles for no purpose; we saw the bullet holes in cars to prove that. It did eventually calm down, but the Congo was never the same again.

Wars and rumours of wars became the order of the day, and shocking incidents took place, which have been recorded elsewhere. There were unpleasant incidents within Zambia too, during that period of unrest. Over-excited people, psyched up by inflammatory orators, became dangerous. Lives were lost in these incidents, including a lady taking her children home from school one day whose car was set on fire. Anne and I, on a shopping visit to town, had our car stoned as we left the town, and in another incident, Anne and our son Brian were caught in tear gas that had been released against rioting students, while they were shopping one day.

Confusion was the cause of most of these incidents, and unfounded rumours could incite people beyond reason. What was of great concern was the fact that criminal elements, for want of a better word, took advantage of the situation and started high-jacking cars, and blatant highway robberies were not unknown. The police seemed to have difficulty in controlling things as they were under much pressure. Close, elderly friends of ours were high-jacked on a lonely road, tied to trees by the roadside and their new Peugeot car stolen. Another friend was held up at pistol point at his own gateway, and his car taken. A third, travelling with his wife and children, was pulled over by gun-waving bandits, but he calmly pulled out a hand-gun from under his seat and shot two of them. He was, so they say, congratulated by the police at the next traffic control point where he reported the incident. Care had to be taken as to when and where you went, and all sections of the community suffered at one time or another. Our tomato buyers who travelled with a lot of cash, always carried a group of their own guards on the backs of their trucks.

It took years for all this to calm down and be brought under control. The ready availability of guns at that time, especially the famous AK47, had much to answer for. They were regarded by some as the easy way to gain riches or settle old scores. Several of my farmer friends and acquaintances lost their lives in attacks on their homes. Gradually, the criminal element turned their attention to poaching as a safer, more sophisticated and lucrative source of illicit income, often encouraged by greedy buyers outside the country.

This all sounds terrible and the question arises, why did we stay and expose ourselves to these dangers? A doctor friend of

ours did send his mother out of the country for this very reason, and set her up in a house in the U.K. She was shortly after
murdered in her own home by a teenager intruder. Where was
safe? The incidents we heard of, and still do on the news bulletins
from reputedly safer countries helped us see things in realistic
terms. It seemed to us that safety and security was in the mind,
our faith, and in our personal relationships with those around
us. It was also in accepting things as they were, and that change
is a factor of life, and that we should not fight or be frightened
of those changes taking place around us.

How should I sum this chapter up? I would say that, in
hindsight, we are very glad to be where we are. We have emerged
from the experiences of our lives with our faculties intact, and
a feeling of richness just in that. Perhaps in the long run we
have made our own contribution to this country, to its present
and future as it has settled down, and where we have enjoyed so
much and whose people we so deeply appreciate, and thus repaid
in some small way what we have received. How have we done
that during those long years? Well, for one thing, we spent our
working lives producing food in a location where it was much
needed and appreciated, while my farmer brothers and cousins
back overseas were just adding to the unwanted food mountains
of the Western World.

There was still more ahead for us: a challenge and an opportunity which filled many years for both of us. The initial thought
of engaging in such a project was almost laughable for the likes of
us, but who were we to judge? Challenges had been the meat and
drink of our lives, and by the Grace of God we had been able to
face them. So, in one sense, the biggest and best was yet to come.

16

SURPRISE, SURPRISE!

"All things work together."

Romans 8:28

When we made the move to Mkushi I sometimes think we, or at least I, had in the back of our minds the thought that once having set everything up—our home, the farm and our daily routine—and all was ticking over nicely, we would begin to slow down a bit, even move into a comfortable sort of semi-retirement. After all, we were in our early fifties, and the farm was a much smaller proposition than those in which I had previously been engaged. We could then have time for other things, not least keeping in closer contact and visiting more frequently with our now scattering family. But that was not to be.

By the time the first seven years had gone by we had comfortably established our home and residence status as part of this new community. Quite a number of our immediate and extended family had become used to the idea of our being there. They had visited from time to time, grown familiar with and enjoyed the community. They had also established connections with some of the different personalities and families on the many farms in the area.

Among those who visited us several times were Anne's sister, Peggy, and her husband, Gordon, who were active in missionary work in the North West. Gordon was a visionary type of person, and by some might have been called impulsive. He certainly thought out of the box, and what he came out with at times in his outspoken way could seem impractical and even crazy. He did not conform to orthodoxy, nor did he allow obvious limitations or difficulties to thwart him, or to slow him down in throwing out challenges or engaging in them himself. He was in the right sense of the term very much a Man of God, and what he felt God was saying to him he just had to pass on. And he did.

At that time, a number of us made up a small group who met on Sundays for Bible Studies, listening to taped messages from elsewhere, or on occasions having a visitor who came to act as our Pastor. Which is what, on this occasion, brought Gordon to Mkushi. He was a compelling speaker. One Sunday evening, after an active day of meetings and discussions, he asked to speak to a few of us, which he did around our dining room table. Without any preamble he said, "I think you people ought to build and open up a secondary school here in Mkushi. You are central in the country, you have the resources and land available, and there is a great need. People serving in Zambia in many different ways are leaving for the sake of their children's education, or having to send their children far away for school."

Nothing had been further from our thoughts, and perhaps we did not take the suggestion seriously at first. Who were we to do such a thing? None of us had the necessary qualifications for such a venture, all of us were very involved in our farms and businesses, and besides that we just would not know where to start. But the seed had been sown, after which Gordon and Peggy returned home.

For nearly a year none of us could shake the idea out of our minds, and if we did the proposition was firmly brought back to us in different ways. We began to make explorations into the how and where. Was this a crazy idea or was it real and possible? There certainly was a need, we could see that.

The story of this school has been told elsewhere, so I will not repeat it here. Suffice to say that under the guidance of qualified advisors and using our own practical skills and resources, a secondary school with fifty pupils and a handful of staff came to be a reality two years later. Twenty-nine years along the road, it now has over four hundred pupils in Primary, Secondary and Sixth form, and a very active outdoor action and adventure centre, all with supporting staff. Pupils have distinguished themselves in the international academic field in world class exams, and done very well in sporting events in South Africa and the U.K. Ex-pupils are now to be found in a number of leading positions in the country and further afield, including a Member of the Zambian Parliament.

For the purpose of this story of our own life experiences, how did all this affect us personally? And what part did we play?

We were just a part of the whole. No single person could claim to be the prime mover in establishing an institution like this. Perhaps the most important factor was for us once more, and perhaps even more than ever before, becoming part of a team, even though we did not all always see things in the same way, or agree in how to get things done. Perhaps that was our strength as we learned to work through differences of opinion, coming to conclusions which then led to action.

First, a Board of Governors was established, bringing in additional expertise and strengths. I was appointed Chairman of this group, a responsibility I held for twenty years. It was a challenging and fulfilling time. It certainly was not just chairing meetings but rather involved everything from supervising building work and the labour force to interviewing and appointing staff.

Planning the layout was fun too, as was initiating staff from overseas into the ways of the country. There were challenging and on odd occasions distressing issues in which we all had to become involved. However, professional leaders were found and appointed, who, with their staff of teachers, administrators, and builders joined the action and established their own teams, so our responsibilities changed. I think the most important thing for Anne and me was to see it all coming into being as an increasingly professional operation, so that we could gradually relinquish our hands-on involvements.

In the early days, Anne was responsible for the domestic team, and for the first year fed about seventy people, pupils and staff, from a tiny farm-house kitchen. She built a great crew and for the first year, if I wanted any lunch, I had to join the mob at the school. Our local people always respond to leadership and she certainly provided that, but she gave much more and to most (staff and children) became known as "Mama" or "Aunty Anne". Of course, there were difficult moments, which had to be dealt with firmly and decisively. Such as when the school cooks, now trained and doing a good job, were found to be running a little operation on the side, making cakes at the school's expense and selling them to the pupils.

For some years, I oversaw the building operations, while my neighbour managed the finance and purchasing of materials. A third neighbour, further away, used his resources and time to establish grounds layout and sports facilities. There were frustrations and setbacks, but incredibly they were overcome. Sometimes things looked dark, and forecasts of gloom and doom were thrown at us. But the ship kept sailing on, pupils were enrolled and finally qualified, terms went by, events happened, and expectations were fulfilled. Chengelo became a fixture and a factor in the educational and family life of Zambia.

We may have put considerable time, thought, energy, and even some resources into the project, but we were rewarded in so many ways. Firstly, it was the pure satisfaction of being part of a team that took on and effectively contributed to the whole. Secondly, it was seeing the school settling firmly into its role of fitting young people for life in the broadest sense. Thirdly, it was the eventful but amazing learning curve for us as we contributed where and when we could. We learned so much: about people, young and old, pupils and staff; about how to get things done by being strongly focused while at the same time wending our way through the intricacies of the regulations, requirements, restrictions and shortages of material that confronted us in our new young country which was still working its own way in becoming an established and viable entity. Perhaps the greatest reward of all was in the friendships and personal contacts we made, parents, pupils, and staff alike as well as others who, apart from the School, we might never have come to know.

On one occasion when I was in the U.K., I was crossing London to catch a train for the North. I stood at Victoria station, feeling and no doubt looking a bit lost as I searched for the correct Underground entrance. I noticed in passing a young lady sitting on her backpack against a wall. She looked straight at me, then got up and came purposefully towards me. She took me by the arm, to my consternation, but then looked me straight in the face and said, "I'm Norma."

This was London and I was from the Zambian bush, thousands of miles away. I froze. A look of concern came over her face and she said, "You don't know me."

A good opening shot I thought so I said, "No, I don't."

"But I'm from Chengelo."

Oh my! She had started the little Primary class, taught my grandson to read, and been in our home many times. Many apologies and much laughter followed, after which she helped me find my way. I have never heard of or seen her since.

On another occasion, an African lady came up to me in Heathrow airport and said, "You are Mr Wyatt?" in an enquiring way. Her son was a pupil at the school.

Nearer home, quite often young folk have come up to us in various places and told us who they were and when they had been at the school, and asked us how we were.

Perhaps some of the closest relationships and friendships we established were with staff. Young couples came from overseas to teach, had their babies, who grew up and started school here; these couples were Anne's specialty. Other older couples, in early retirement from the U.K., became close friends. Most of all were the younger folk, away from home for the first time and a little lost at first, who found a place they could relax and be comfortable in an informal way. Some of them became much like a part of our extended family; we met their parents and even stayed with them when we were in the U.K. ourselves.

There were times when we, out of necessity, became substitute parents and a haven for young folk who found the going hard. Perhaps we helped them but they all contributed so much to our lives, and gave us a new and widening content, especially as our own family were spreading further in the world. Sunday lunches were a factor in all this as our large dining table was filled, and many a fat leg of lamb was flattened in one sitting on these fun occasions. This would lead on to Sunday afternoon walks, and tea with chocolate cake.

Slowly we withdrew from the action, perhaps "stood back" is a better term. The school had become firmly established and was running on its own impetus. We live only ten minutes' drive away from the campus, so maintained our contacts. Anne relinquished her role in the domestic side of things, although her old staff still came to see her and tell her of their troubles. After twenty years, I retired from the Board of Governors and its Chairmanship. New blood was needed and they came on board with new ideas and new approaches to cope with the ever-changing staff. I felt my time at that level was over; I needed a new role.

As a Trustee, which is a lifetime commitment, both Anne and I keep close contact with the school and staff, and to this day I pop in now and again to have half an hour with the Principal or one of the Heads, discussing one issue or another. For so many years it has been a major part of our lives, and I suppose it always will be to the end. If it hadn't been for this challenge so long ago we might have stagnated, or even become bored, a thing I have never been, at least since I left school.

But what was the real motivation behind Chengelo School, and what kept it on track? Neither of us have any doubt but that it was the hand of God. It was He who gave us the challenge through Gordon; it was He who showed us the way to do something that materially and humanly speaking was impossible. It was He who kept us on track, who lifted us up when we were down, and showed us the way when we could have got it wrong. It was He who sent us the right staff members at the right time. And in so many ways it could only have been God who was behind the miraculous ways in which problems and difficulties were overcome. None of us who were involved—and I take the liberty of speaking for others as well—would want to or even could have the audacity to take the credit for this amazing work of God right here on our doorstep. We might have played a role in it all, but only that. The credit is given to Whom it belongs. When I visit the school, walk around and talk to people, I am so glad to have been a part of it all.

I sometimes ask myself this: what if we had laughed the whole idea off right at the start, had said it was impossible and crazy as some onlookers did? What if we had folded under the pressures or dwelt on our many limitations? What if we had even said we were too busy, or had too many other commitments already? It would have affected so many people, denied so many young people the opportunities Chengelo has given them, influenced family lives as parents would have had to leave Zambia to get their children educated elsewhere and in doing so their service would have been lost to Zambia. It would have denied many support workers of employment, as they contributed to the building and running of the school.

However, I think we, the start-up team, would have been the greatest losers. I thank God that He gave us the courage—and we did need it at times—to ignore the impossibilities and just go for it. In so doing, we gained a fulfilment, a richness and a grateful sense of satisfaction which otherwise we would never have experienced. I can't speak for others but only for ourselves, but I think we, the start-up team, were the ones to gain the most. All we had done was what we could do and were capable of. No less and no more. Frankly, we were surprised to discover this had a wider, deeper effect than we had ever imagined possible.

Later years; with Anne on a visit to what was once the Wyatt family farm in West Sussex

With our son, Brian

Brian and Gayle

Turn left for Kapanda Farm: a new start

*Kapanda House.
Our Family Home for
the last 37 years*

Our family at a gathering for my 60th birthday, 1987.
From left to right: *Helen, Liz, Brian, Anne, me, Sheila, and Julia*

With some of our grandchildren, now grown men and women

*With President Mwanawasa and the eight Chengelo Duke of Edinburgh
Gold awardees of the year, November 2006*

Our family at a gathering for my 70th birthday, December 1997.
From left to right: *Sheila, Helen, me, Anne, Julia, Brian and Liz*

*With our five children, sons- and daughter-in-law, and 14
grandchildren, 1997*

A visit to my father's farm, a place of many youthful memories

With Anne, 2006

17

HERE AND THERE: SPECIFIC INCIDENTS AND SPECIAL PEOPLE

"The Lord shall preserve your going out and your coming in."

Psalm 121:8

At different times and in differing situations there have been a number of significant happenings that have occurred to us in which special people have played a part. Yet they seem to me to have been a measure of the whole, and deserve a special mention and chapter of their own.

I often think of them, and memories when recalled can be very live and special, as so many of them have contributed greatly to the challenges, surprises, experiences and even fun, all have which have made life so rich. So yes, they stand on their own but at the same time slot into the overall life and times which I have enjoyed so much.

So, at this point, my faithful reader, if you have got this far, I offer them to you as they stand.

During the 1960's, while we were living and working at Hillwood, we experienced some years of heavy and continuous rain. Rainfall is always higher in the North Western part of the country, where there are many smaller rivers and streams feeding the larger ones to cope with the run off. These swell tremendously to flood level at times, and the wooden bridges get lifted off their cradles and swept away. Consequently, roads were closed, cutting us off from the outside world.

I have also seen the water table so high and the earth so soaked that water would bubble out of the ground in the middle of the road, turning it into a quagmire. This usually happened in February towards the climax of the rains, after which the roads eventually dried off through April and May. But it would be May and even June before this flood peak reached the Victoria Falls, which would then become an even more glorious, roaring spectacle.

One year, during February, my brother-in-law Paul travelled to the Copperbelt to buy stocks of urgently needed supplies, taking our only lorry. While he was there, the bridge across the Mwombeji River was washed away. He heard over the Missionary Radio Network that there was no way for him cross it in order to return home, so he sent me a telegram asking me to meet him at the *Mwombeji* Mission Station. The idea was that he would get to the Mission from the Copperbelt side and together we would somehow transfer the essential goods across the flooded river, and take them home from there. The "how" we would decide when the time came; one can always make a plan in Zambia.

I hired a lorry from another trader and set off. However, about ten miles before I reached the Mwombeji, I found another bridge over a smaller river had also been washed away. I managed to cross over that one on foot fairly easily, leaving the lorry there. Hiring a bicycle from a chap in a nearby village, I cycled the remaining ten miles to the Mwombeji, arriving in the late afternoon.

Now the challenge was to cross this swollen river and walk up the hill to the Mission Station where I imagined Paul would be waiting. As always in Zambia, the country of optimists, there was someone to hear my story and who willingly agreed to not only show me the best way but to escort me across the river. As we set off into the bush to the crossing point he knew of, his perky young wife announced that she was coming too.

Soon we arrived at a fairly narrow point where the current was very fast. What now? Laid across it, from bank to bank, were two long poles about as thick as my leg, and the man started to cross over on these without hesitation, one foot on each pole—an amazing balancing feat. To my astonishment, as soon as he reached the opposite bank, his little wife hitched up her skirts and followed him. I had no choice but to follow suit.

I took off my shoes for a start and threw them across: step one, a point of no return. Then, with great care and deliberation I set out, one foot on each pole. However, as I weighed more than both the man and his wife combined the poles sank down into the water, which came swirling with all its force halfway up my calves. I was afraid to lift my feet up to step forward as the pole would spring back up too, and it would have been a high stepping exercise. Instead, I slid my feet along the pole, desperately trying to keep my balance, and in this way miraculously reached the other side. I calmly sat down and put on my shoes, trying to make out as if I did this sort of thing every day. We set off once more and within a few minutes came to another, much wider, larger river.

"What river is this?" I asked.

"The Mwombeji," I was told.

"So, what was that one behind us?"

"Ah, that was *mwanindi*, its child."

Oh no!

Here, poles were laid across the swiftly running water from the bank where we stood to a tree in the middle of the river, but this time with the refinement of a hand rail on which to hold. We repeated the crossing feat, and eventually found ourselves perched in the tree with the river rushing all around us. We held on grimly as the tree swung this way and that, pushed about by the strong current.

"What now?" I asked; there was still half the river to cross.

"The poles have gone," I was told, "The river has taken them. We can go no further."

By this time, it was almost dark and there we were, clustered closely together, perched in the tree like large birds. There was nothing for it; we had to retreat, which we did, repeating the whole performance in reverse as it grew darker by the minute. But we made it. My two companions showed absolutely no fear and were quite matter-of-fact about it all. I wish I could say the same for myself. I am a poor swimmer, and if I had lost my balance I would have been at the mercy of the river.

Now what?

"It's alright," said the young man, unfazed. "We can try again tomorrow. You can sleep in my shop tonight."

And I did, on the counter, with a mattress and blankets from his selling stock on the shelf which he cheerfully pulled down for me. As I settled down, hungry and frustrated, it began to rain. A flock of goats took refuge on the veranda, banging against the door and walls. The father goat, or perhaps two, seemed to spend a busy night checking out his wives with a hearty billy-goat bleating, and there was constant shuffling and bumping. It was not a good night.

Next day, we did it all again—this time replacing the lost poles—and made it across both rivers without mishap. I was getting good at the dangerous trapeze act. Safely on the far side of the Mwombeji, I walked up the hill to find the couple who lived at the Mission. Of my brother-in-law there was no sign. The couple were old friends and I told them my story; then, while the lady fed me a good breakfast, her husband got on the radio network to track down Paul and the lorry. The report came back that because of the bad roads and uncertainty, he had decided to take an alternative but much longer route through the Congo. All my heroic stunts were for nothing. I would just have to retrace my steps—balancing act, ten-mile cycle ride and all—and drive home.

Paul arrived there before me. I must admit, I was not amused. But I can still picture that brave young woman, her skirts as high as she needed without a care, nonchalantly stepping out onto those poles ahead of me over the rushing water, and then sitting with her man and myself as we held tightly together on the swaying tree in the middle of the main river. All without a word of complaint or fear. She deserved a medal.

* * *

Many of the memorable incidents in our experiences were related to road travel. I have, over seventy years, driven many hundreds of thousands of miles—or kilometers as we now measure them—on highways, motorways, main routes, side roads, district roads (mostly dirt tracks), off-road, and no roads at all across fields and through the bush. I've driven in sheeting rain, axle-deep mud, slippery and icy conditions, deep sand, and thick dust. And all of this in every kind of vehicle: Mercedes sedans, two-by-four Pick-up trucks, Land Rovers, four-by-four-wheel drive Toyotas, and a rickety Morris van with twelve-inch wheels, not to mention trucks and lorries of various sizes, loaded, over-loaded and empty. For ten weeks, while living in Chingola and trying to earn some extra money, I worked on an earth-moving project driving Caterpillar scrapers and Bull Dozer D 8's. I drove twelve-hour shifts from six to six with a fifteen-minute food break, one week during the day, the following week through the night.

Many of our road trips entailed anything up to twelve hours' continuous travel with very short necessity breaks, Anne passing out food and drink as we went. One trip in South Africa was sixteen hours long (we got lost in Pretoria), taking the kids to school.

Three instances stand out in all this. One was driving a missionary lady friend of ours and her two children for just over one hundred and twenty miles to her Mission Station home in the dark. I had planned to travel the same road with a lorry, but she asked if I would drive her car as she was not that confident in the conditions. She was a lovely person, coming from Chattanooga in the South of the U.S.A., with a wonderful southern accent. She wanted to get home to her husband who would be worrying about her.

It was dark, and the rain was sheeting down in such torrents that the beams from the headlights reflected off the rain and blinded us. The road was cambered, sloping down on each side, and the only way I knew we were driving off centre was when the car tilted one way or the other. Fortunately, there was no other traffic or obstructions, and we made it safely to her home. During that same night, our lorry driver pulled in two or three hours after us, having driven through the same weather. This road was notorious for collapsing under wet conditions, as it did not follow the high ground water shed all the way.

On another occasion, with my brother-in-law and ten workmen well equipped with axes, shovels and ropes, it took us nineteen hours to cover one hundred miles of this same road. The men pushed or towed us by hand through some of the worst parts, the water knee-deep in places. Twice, we were forced to leave the road altogether, cutting a track through the bush. With the men pulling on the ropes and the wheels skidding and digging through the soaking ground, we travelled for about half a mile around an impassable stretch blocked by other trucks sunk deep in the mud and stagnant water.

It was always a matter of assessing the conditions, working out the possibilities, and then doing whatever would work best. Lying under a lorry in the rain and dark, jacking up the wheels, first one side and then the other, pushing timber cut from the surrounding bush under them to give a firm grip, and laying more poles as decking ahead, was all part of the job.

* * *

One amusing incident that comes to mind was when I was taking Anne's sister, Peggy, and her little boy to meet her husband. It was a wet journey but the road was firm. As we travelled, we came upon a small bus or People Carrier stopped by the road with a flat tyre. Beside it stood a white-clad Nun, with a small jack in her hand and a puzzled look on her face. We stopped; I removed my shoes and socks, pulled a waterproof over my head, and got out.

"Can I help you?" I asked. A silly question.

In the vehicle were about ten young Nuns, novices I guessed, and I politely requested that they all got out to lighten the vehicle. Fortunately, the rain had stopped for a bit so they did, and I crept under the vehicle with my own larger car jack. The axle seemed a long way under, but I managed to reach it, scrape soft soil out to a hard spot, and raise the heavy vehicle.

I then crept out again to look for the spare wheel, and found myself surrounded by a bunch of giggling girls (all in Nuns Habits) and their Mother Superior, who was trying not to laugh as well. Wheel changed, I had to reverse the process to remove the jack. By this time, I was thoroughly wet and dirty, but the vehicle was useable again. The dear Mother Superior not only thanked me but blessed me kindly, with the young girls trying hard to look the part. They seemed to be a really nice bunch.

"Please go carefully," I urged. "You have no spare tyre now." And we went on our way.

"What were those girls laughing at?" I asked Peggy.

She explained that they had been staring in wonder at my oversized feet and long, bare legs sticking out from under the bus, as that was all they could see of me. One of them had made a remark (probably quite un-Nun like) which had set them all off giggling. I do hope they made it that day, and in later days fulfilled their dreams and vocations.

* * *

In all my travels, I was one day taken completely by surprise and jettisoned into a situation of which I had no forewarning, nor had I been aware of the imminent danger. It was early one New Year's Day, and we were driving from Lusaka to a wedding in Kitwe on the Copperbelt, a journey of several hours. Anne had gone on ahead in our Toyota Corolla with Brian and Julia; I was behind in a Toyota Crown station wagon with Sheila and Helen, her little dog, Heidi, and the luggage with all our wedding clothes packed in the back.

It was raining quite hard, but I didn't think that was a problem. However, at a well-known spot on a slight bend, Landless Corner, it suddenly seemed as though my car became airborne. The steering wheel was totally unresponsive, and the car seemed to be gliding and out of control. We slid across the road to our right, and off onto the grassy verge. As soon as we were off the tar surface of the road, the vehicle made earth contact again, and we somersaulted end over end several times before coming to a crashing halt, right side up. It was all over in seconds, it seemed. We managed to climb out intact and were amazingly able to walk away, although pretty dazed by what had happened. Looking at the car, now in a smashed and squashed-up heap, I could only say that we had survived by the goodness of Almighty God.

A young man from the nearby farm took us back into Lusaka, and to a hospital. Sheila had lost the tip of her index finger and a lot of blood, and was the most in shock. Helen was pretty bruised but had been held down by the luggage in the back, which had pushed her seat forward and pinned her on the floor. My glasses were broken, and Helen's little dog, Heidi, who had been on her twice-yearly heat, returned to normal with the shock (and never had another heat in her life). Anne, of course knew nothing, and had driven on to Kitwe. We phoned from Lusaka to the house where they had gone to change into smarter clothes to tell her what had happened; they had no choice but to attend the wedding without us and in the clothes they had on.

I later learned from the insurance agent that we must have hydroplaned. When more water builds up against a tyre than it can scatter, the resulting water pressure in front of the wheel forces a thin but even sheet of water under the tyre, causing it to separate from the road surface and lose traction. Hydroplaning is a phenomenon that has even been known to cause aircraft landing in the rain on smooth runways to crash, and in our case, it made sense as there was a build-up of rain water running across the road at that particular spot. I was quite unaware of this hazard at the time, but have been very conscious of it ever since when travelling in rainy conditions. In fact, I prefer and look for a rougher part of the road surface at such times to travel on, as I have no desire to repeat that experience.

* * *

In all our travels, we have met many good people and have often been helped and given overnight hospitality, sometimes at short notice. There seemed to be a camaraderie of the road, and in early days a chance meeting with another vehicle would call for a social stop and a quickly made cup of tea. I have cooked breakfast on the side of the road and shared it with other passing travelers more than once. We once towed home a Bavarian couple we found broken down by the roadside, and they happily stayed the night with their two small children, while father fixed the car in our workshop.

On another occasion as we were going to bed we heard a car drive up. I went out with a torch to find an elderly couple in a small, open truck loaded with books and literature for mission distribution. They had no waterproof cover and it was just beginning to rain. Quickly we got the vehicle under cover, and these folks into the house; beds were soon made up, and these lovely if rather naïve people stayed as our guests. We sent them on their way the next day, a little better equipped to cope with the rain. They became valued friends, and we came to appreciate their commitment to their mission work in remote places.

Travel, with all its tedium, hazards, fun, interest and joys, was a part of our life. In early days, it was taken in two-seater light farm trucks, or Pick-ups as we called them. The smaller children would be tucked in front with us, while the older ones would lie in the open back, covered with blankets and waterproofs and probably accompanied by a dog or two who loved this style of travel.

In later days, we travelled more comfortably, making leisurely trips in our second-hand Mercedes sedan through Botswana to South Africa on holiday, or full-day trips to Zimbabwe to see family and the children in school. Our many different cars, still remembered with affection, were very much part of the family, and when no longer able to cope and exchanged for something more reliable, were greatly missed and mourned.

The children learned to be good travelers and cope with the long days, and how to make full use of the stops along the way. And as with life in general, one never quite knew what might be waiting just around the corner. On one occasion, when the School bus bringing our girls back from Zimbabwe (then Rhodesia) for the holidays failed to arrive on time, I drove towards the Border to look for it. There it was, broken down on the side of the road, the driver asleep in his seat while waiting for help, and about twenty or so school girls dancing in the road to the music from one of their radios. It was near midnight. Fortunately, traffic was scarce that night.

Today, roads are being upgraded with the latest hard surface, travel is much faster, and distances are measured in hours rather than days. A lot of the fun and challenge has gone out of travel, but such is progress, and there is always a cost.

18

FUNDAMENTALS, OR WHAT MAKES ME TICK

"I know whom I have believed."

2 Timothy 1:12

Some years back, I was attending a Cattle Field Day Demonstration to which I had taken a couple of our pedigree cows for demonstration purposes. I was carrying what is commonly known as a thumb stick, a thin stick with a forked end, which is used for touching the feet of the animal to get it to stand properly (it must, of course, be trained to respond!). During a pause in the day's proceedings I was standing aside, leaning on my stick, when a good farmer friend beside me said quietly, "You even look like Moses now." A quiet dig and a bit of fun; no problem.

At another cattle farming Field Day, a few of us were chatting between ourselves and talking over problems we had to face and overcome. After I had shared my piece in the conversation another farmer startled me by saying in all seriousness, "But you have God with you, don't you?"

The questions are, "Do I? And if so, why me? Why should I, even in fun, be compared to that great Man of God, Moses? And why should I, as the second remark seems to indicate, have an edge in resolving everyday problems?" These questions deserve serious answers, and I believe my story would be incomplete if I did not attempt to provide some.

It is not original to say that there are factors and features that we absorb when we are young that remain a part of us into our later years. They may be from the environment in which we are raised; they may be cultural or class prejudices, or even national or racial fixations. Certainly, for me, family background, lifestyle and beliefs as well as loyalties and the overall order of life have had an ongoing effect on me throughout my life—mostly for good. I can see clearly now, as I look back over a span of the sixty years since I left home and launched out on my own, how the influence of my early years and home life have remained with me, and I find an increasing desire to hark back to them as time passes. Further, I realise how valuable they are to me, and I can only express my gratitude to my parents who held fast for us all and gave us clear signals while we were under their influence and control.

The learning curve, as it is so often called, consists of not only taking on board these issues, but also in the slower process of realising their rightness, or wrongness in some cases as some folk may feel. The question is, why? How did this come about for me? What was my learning curve in this area?

As usual, to find the answer to most tough questions one has to go back to the beginning, and I must in all honesty do that now, in order to give a clear picture as I see it at this time.

I was raised in what some would call a religious home and environment; the popular term was a "Christian Home". While it was orderly and there were clear and definite do's and don'ts, I believe it was far more than that. In fact, I have come to the understanding that mere "religion" can be quite barren and mind-less. It was (and I am sure my siblings would agree) a Christian home and environment in the right and true sense of the word, where Christian principles and truths were upheld, taught and observed. Some of these were in the outward form: grace before meals, family prayers, and Sunday observance as "The Lord's day" when attendance at Church Services and Sunday School were the norm.

Family prayers were special. Dad would read a portion from the Bible and we would all then kneel, with much scraping of chairs on the floor, while Dad prayed. He did so earnestly and meaningfully in the Bible language of the King James Version, covering a wide area from the daily work and needs to our Grandparents "in their declining years" and, without fail, "Thine ancient people, the Jews". I can still hear his distinct voice rising and falling as he earnestly called on God.

Perhaps his prayers were a bit stereotyped but were very sincere nevertheless, and this prayer time took precedence over all else. His dog had it all worked out and knew when the end was coming. As Dad prayed "Lord, bless us today, and make us a blessing," the dog got up, shook himself and went and stood by the door, ready for the "Amen" and for it to be opened in our rush for school.

No farm work was done on Sundays apart from caring for livestock; bad language was not used or tolerated, and there was a strong work ethic of duty and caring. The fact that we, as individuals, were not our own but bought with the price of the sacrifice of Jesus Christ, the Son of the Living God, was clearly stated in two beautiful paintings depicting Biblical quotes, done by our gifted Grandma Wyatt. These paintings were displayed in our family dining room, and any who came as guests to sit at our table could see this unashamed statement of the family's faith.

This was the home foundation of our lives. It was based on a decision—so my mother told me later—made by our parents in their early married life that they would honour God in every way, follow the pathway of Christian living so clearly laid down in the Scriptures, and raise their children in the fear and under-standing of the Lord. There it was, and I took it all for granted as the norm. As a child, it gave me a sense of security. God took care of me and Jesus loved me; what more could I ask?

But, and maybe there is always a but, as I moved towards my teens I realised two things. The first was that I personally did not always measure up to these standards and truths in either understanding or behaviour. The second was that many others—like the parents of my school friends—while being nice, kind people, did not regard them at all as important as my parents did. I was a bit confused, and was being pulled two ways in my thinking. I wanted to follow the path and go the way of my Mum and Dad; they were good people and I admired them, especially Dad, but there was an exciting world out there from which I had been shielded and even warned, but which was very attractive.

What I had not realised was that although it was good to follow the example and standards of my parents and perhaps bask in their reputation and shelter under them, there was the need for me to make a personal decision and commitment for myself. That was if I wanted to and if I was going to make any fist of it.

Through my teens, I worked and worried through this seesaw of understanding and direction, but (and I'm not trying to sound pious in saying this) it was through the goodness and grace of God that I did not totally go the opposite path beyond a point of no return. Although I did dabble in it a bit. I was helped and guided through this seeming dilemma in the contacts I had with others who so kindly took an interest and had a concern for me.

Superficially (and I emphasise that) as I matured into my late teens and early twenties, I was accepted as a well-established Christian believer, who had made the Lord his God. I ticked the boxes of my outward profession of faith, and I may say earnestly and honestly, I made every endeavour to live up to it. The crunch was that in doing this I was taking God for granted. I had honoured Him outwardly, so I felt, so He must honour me by giving me success and a position in life which I felt was my due. I had some hard lessons to learn, and in the tough course of life what I felt was my due was withheld from me, and as I see it now I was allowed to make my own mistakes.

At that time, I felt my prayers, which were a bit sketchy I must admit, were not being answered. The answers were there all right, but in the negative. I had to learn that God is always there, that He always answers prayer, and that "No", in whatever form it comes, can be the answer, even if it is not to our personal liking. Dad used to say if you don't make mistakes you don't make anything, and to add to that I discovered you don't learn anything either.

As I have written in previous chapters, failures began to show up in my farming life, and things did not work out at all to my liking and expectations. But, and this is what I want to convey, the guiding hand of God was always there in whatever situation I found myself, even if I could not see it. He was continually there to protect, to lead, to give understanding, to guard me and my family. It took me years to fully realise this and see the evidence of it. As we moved from one situation to another there was always something new He had for us: new challenges we had to face up to, new stands we had to make, how to be strong and upright.

In the terms of the Psalms, I came to learn in a practical way that it was He who was always our strength and our shield, our rock and hiding place. My understanding of Him and His ways grew and became clearer as time went by. He gradually became more real in our lives, and it were His ways, His path, His principles and standards that had to be—and eventually proved to be—the keyway to a more successful and effective life. And the closer we walked with God (to use that term) the more effective and secure our lives became.

I now know this, in fact two things: firstly, that however long we may live, life never ceases to be a learning curve, both in the smallest details of life and in the greatest things; and secondly, that the key to ensuring a steady upward trend in that curve, although there may be a few dips here and there, is in our understanding and our relationship with God. It was for me, and I don't believe it just happens. The Bible says that "Those who seek me find Me." It also teaches that He is not that far from us, even if we don't recognise or realize it.

So, perhaps as a summary, I had to find the course myself and then stay steady on it. Problems there were, problems there still are, but the means of handling them are also there at hand. I must now admit that, after a life time of seeking and finding, I still don't know all the answers; but I do know where they lay, and I can and do without reserve put my faith in the living God. Not as easy as it sounds, especially after a lifetime of dealing with challenges and solving problems for myself as part of my job and responsibilities.

I have now retired, both of us have, from active farming and other responsibilities. I cannot foretell the future, but I can relax in the security that it is all in good hands. If only I had done that at an earlier age perhaps we might have avoided some of the challenges and traumas that came our way.

While I am writing this, I can imagine being asked "What Church do you belong to?" The answer is "I don't," not formally anyway to any of the long list of recognised Church Denominations that have come into being in the Western World. I have never been Christened, Baptised, Confirmed, Inducted, or officially welcomed or made a member of any particular denomination of the Christian Church. I am not a Roman Catholic, nor an Anglican, a Baptist, Pentecostal or any other. As children, we attended Sunday School in the village Free Baptist Chapel; our family involvement was with a Christian Brethren Fellowship in the nearest town, a two hundred strong group where my father was an elder. I went to an Anglican boarding school where we had a free choice of what Sunday morning Service we could attend in the town; I went to the Free Church where my school friend's father was Minister, an imposing building in a prominent position in the town.

In the course of my life, I have attended and been a part of functions in many different churches, and have benefited from spiritual input right across the board. I greatly admire the evangelist, Dr Billy Graham, and also the current Pope. One of my favourite devotional books was written by a Catholic Priest, and another was written by a South African farmer. Our present spiritual home, or Church as some would call it, is a very open fellowship made up of folk from many different backgrounds, and led by four farmers who are devoted to God and the service of the group. I have in the past been what is termed an elder of such a group myself, but am now content to be led by younger men.

I hold that we all as Believers have a responsibility to fulfil the gifts and abilities with which God has endowed us. I have tried to do this willingly and as best I can. Consequently, I have been asked to lead a number of ceremonies including funerals and even a wedding (at 48 hours' notice when the Minister previously arranged pulled out). I have spoken—some would call it preached but I prefer the word shared—many times in various Churches as and when asked.

Incidentally, I am a bit reluctant to use the term "Christian" as it has rather lost its definitive meaning. So often now-a-days it is used to define a culture or even political standing rather than Believers in and followers of Jesus Christ. Sadly, there are many who would regard themselves as under the Christian umbrella but who could hardly be called either Believers in or followers of Jesus Christ. On the other hand, I find that there are true and simple Believers who do not belong to or go to a Church of any kind. It is worth noting that the term Believers is a Biblical one, and these initial folks were first called Christians as a sort of loose nickname in a heathen city.

The question might well be asked of me, "Did you ever have any doubts?" I would be dishonest to say "No". I reckon there is no harm in questioning ourselves, and answering the challenge, "Do I really believe what I say I believe?" But doubts must be dealt with, not allowed to take root or destroy.

The answer came to me early one morning just a few years back, when I woke with the terrible feeling that there was no God, that the whole concept of a Mighty God was false, He just was *not*. What was hugely significant to me was the feeling that came with it: one of horror, of a massive vacuum, of meaninglessness and hollowness. It seemed as though if there was no God at all, then there was nothing else either. To my intense relief, this inner but very real and horrific feeling passed as I fully awoke and came to my senses. I shared all this that very day at our Church Fellowship gathering, and to my surprise a lady responded by saying she had had exactly the same experience.

But this is the issue; the total absence of an Almighty and everlasting God, creator and upholder of the whole universe, is more unthinkable and illogical than is His very real existence and involvement, whether in space and time or just in my little and insignificant life; and it's much harder to explain. Even non-believers, atheists, acknowledge God because by my reasoning, if they did not, why do they go to the trouble of not believing and emphasising their non-belief of something that does not exist to them anyway?

I found there is more than one approach to the whole concept of a great, amazing and loving God whom we acknowledge and in whom I believe. One way is blind faith, just that: accepting all that we have heard and read about Him, taking it at its face value. There is also the way of taking it as an optional extra, grateful there is a God in the background to pick up the pieces, but not including Him or regarding His real presence as a part of everyday life. The other, and most rewarding way is recognising and including God and all that He has to offer and all He does, in our everyday lives, as much or more than the closest member of our family.

C. S. Lewis, one of the great intellectuals of the last century and author of the Narnia books and many others, came to realise the reality of God by a deep intellectual process of reasoning and conclusion, and was astonished at the simplicity and reward of it all, as he lays out in his book, "Surprised by Joy". Others come to the same conclusion by a simpler route, seeing the evidence of God's presence in their own home, family, and even garden: the process of life and growth, the biological miracles all around us, the way in which, spurred on by temperature and moisture, everything springs to life. The evidence of an unseen hand is right outside our doors.

To Greek intellectuals of his day, the Apostle Paul simplified the reality of what they regarded as an "unknown God".

He reminded them that "in Him we live and move and have our being". Biologists may be able to explain *how* it works, but they cannot tell us *why* it works. This question is posed by God Himself, in talking to the famous Job, "Who makes the hinds to calve?"

I am a simple man. I have read some of C. S. Lewis's books, and although I see what he is getting at I cannot always understand or follow his reasoning. Perhaps I am, because of my calling in life, more akin to the "Old Herbaceous" common-or-garden approach, expressed by the old Welsh lady I met years ago, straight from the Valleys of her country: "He looks after me as though I were His only child, He does." Or the simple acceptance of an Almighty God in whose hands are time and eternity, life and death, times and seasons, as expressed in simple but challenging verses coming from the mouth of an unpretentious English countryman and farm worker. I love them, as they bring together Earth and Heaven.

"*The mists be on the river bed,*
The roses all be gone;
And here be I, about to die,
With Harvest coming on.
Dear Lord, I've traipsed some weary miles,
I'll be main glad to rest awhiles.

The folk'll soon be in the fields
A-getting in the grain;
For most of those, the time You've chose
Be awkward in the main.
Though not so bad, 'tis sure, for they
As be a-workin' by the day.

September be a better month
For all the carter men;
And when I die don't signify,
So let I bide till then

The wagons'll be standing by,
And there'll be time to bury I."
From Green Fingers Again, by Reginald Arkell

Going back to where I started in this section of my tale, I can confidently say my belief and faith in my God, first rooted in my childish understanding and then growing into a basic foundation and reality, has been fundamental throughout my life. There have been failures, there have been doubts, there have been wavering and weak spots. I have done some unwise things and made foolish decisions of which I'm not very proud. But I *am* proud to say this—and I dare to say it—that my God, whom I try to honour as my father did, has been the ultimate Guide and the one fixed point of my life, the secure base on which I can build and to which I have been able to return when veering off course, the One on whose shoulders I can cry, and the One to whom I can hold fast, no matter what the situation might be.

It is not religion; it is not a ritual; it is not just "rightness". It is an ongoing and very secure relationship. And all the credit goes to our God.

19

PEOPLE, WEALTH AND VALUES

"His children and their children to the fourth generation."

Job 42:16

At one stage of my life, I was confined to my bed in hospital in Pretoria, South Africa. I had been through some tricky and life-threatening procedures, and our four daughters had come and were supporting their mother, all staying in Sheila's home in Midrand. They would come to see me during visiting hours, sometimes one or two at a time, at others, altogether. This seemed to impress the ward nurses who were mostly Zulu or Twsana girls, and one of them asked me how big our family was. I told her the sum of our children, grandchildren, and their children—the whole lot. A smile spread across her face and she exclaimed, "Oh my, you are rich!" How right she was; large families in their culture mean wealth and security.

I repeated this incident to my brother later, and in return he reminded me of an incident that took place in a very different cultural setting. It was the habit of farmers and butchers in the area where I was raised in the U.K. to meet up at the local cattle

southeastern

St Mary Cray Station

=== CARD PAYMENT ===

Sayes Court Road
Orpington
BR5 2PQ
AID:A0000000031010
Visa Debit
Card: ****************0268
Pan Seq Nr: 01
ICC
SALE
Amount :
GBP124.50
PIN VERIFIED
Auth: 526960
Ref: 029048
Merchant: ***78081
TID: ****0491
41788724A0BD5BB8 40
Date: 27/12/19 Time: 07:12:00

CARDHOLDER COPY
PLEASE RETAIN FOR YOUR RECORDS

Card Payment Ref: 2414910044333

507310IW30M1491 7795 2670 07:11 27-12-19

THANK YOU FOR YOUR CUSTOM
AND TRAVELLING WITH SOUTHEASTERN
www.southeasternrailway.co.uk

market on a Monday morning for selling, buying, doing business deals, and so on. It was also an opportunity to exchange news. On this particular occasion, the talking point was of the death of one of their number. Inevitably the question was asked: "What did he leave?" which was viewed as a measure of past success.

"He left eighteen thousand pounds," was the answer.

A pause while the men gathered round digested this vital bit of news. Then a bluff and serious man spoke.

"What did you say he did with it?"

"He left it!" came the answer.

"Well, that didn't do him much good, did it?"

As usual this raises questions. How do we measure wealth? And, where or in what form are our values? I met a man once who thought of everything in terms of money, ready cash. He told me that he even evaluated his own time by the hour and seemed to infer that time not spent in business, which for him was making money, was lost time. This seemed to include the time he spent talking to me!

So often I have heard folk describe a person as being "successful", and what they usually mean is that they have, through business or by a manner of business-style rating, either made a lot of money or are earning a high salary. Of course, when engaged in business in any form it is incumbent upon one to manage that business in such a way that it is effective and prosperous, either by growth or by profitability. However, doing so at all costs—a very wide term—is not acceptable and can lead to ruin in other ways.

A friend of my father's, who was a successful business man, once wrote to me in referring to my own activities: "Russell, it is not the income that matters, but the outcome." Perhaps at this stage of my life it would be helpful if I spent more time looking at the outcome of my life and work.

For a start I can, and do, look at the farm (now in the capable hands of Alex who is married to our granddaughter Nikki), the farm on which we have spent thirty-seven years and where we are now retired and comfortable in our old home. I see well-bred and productive cattle grazing in pastures, generations down from where I started the cattle breeding years ago. I see a contented and loyal workforce, who are not just farm workers but a faithful part of our wider family. I see things I have developed, but also other things I might have done but did not, for one reason or another. That's the farm.

A bit wider than that are our circle of friends and acquaintances, people I have come to know through the years, and who have shown us friendship and taken an interest in us and our family, as we have taken an interest in theirs. Kindly folk who have shown us caring concern and support. So invaluable to know they are still there, as they are a valuable asset that adds to our sense of well-being.

Then there are the projects and organisations in which we have been involved in the past. To see them functioning well and thriving is tremendously gratifying. I attended a function at one of these organizations recently. I had been a Council member for years and chairman for a period. Hardly anyone knew me that day, but it was very gratifying to see it prospering and providing the services for which it had been structured.

Far more than all this is our immediate family. To picture them now, our four daughters and daughter-in-law who undergird us with their loving care; our ten fine grandsons and four lovely granddaughters all functioning well in their chosen and motivated lives. It sometimes surprises even us to see them all as adults, now facing their own responsibilities and challenges. Our nine great-grandsons and three great-granddaughters are happy, healthy little children, growing and developing into their lives with enthusiasm and purpose, each with their own significant personalities. How lucky and blessed we are!

These are the assets we have; this is the valued outcome of our long lives. This is our true wealth, and in evaluating our lives to our astonishment but also to our satisfaction, we can echo the words of the nurse, "Yes. Oh my! We are rich." And at the same time raise our thanks to God, that He in His goodness has prospered us in all these areas.

When I left England, I turned my back on the welfare State and Society, even on the community security in which I had been raised, although I am sure I did not realise it at the time. I came to a country and situation where there was not only opportunity for personal initiative but where, if one was going to make any effective fist of life at all, it was essential. There was room to make mistakes, which I did in plenty. But there was also room to overcome them, and as I have learned, failure at any one time is not the end but rather a wonderful starting point for learning, recovery and overcoming.

Dependence in any form, I have noted, breeds more dependence and dulls initiative. Independence motivates initiative and encourages a sense of responsibility and desire for progress. My father taught me that.

When I was fourteen he said to me: "Now you are able to work on the farm in your school holidays you are to write down your hours. I will pay you one shilling an hour. That will be your own money from which to buy what you want, including any clothes other than school uniforms and needs. I will pay those, and all your school fees, uniform and other needs, and of course you will be living at home so will have no living expenses."

I returned to school that September with £11.00 pocket money, which I had earned and hoarded with care. At the end of term, I still had ten pounds to take home for Christmas shopping. From then on, I was independent (or so I thought, but it was a good start).

Today we are still independent financially, and while classified Old Age Pensioners (OAP) in English terms because of our age, that is not totally accurate because there is no "P"!

The Apostle Paul spent the last years of his life chained to a Roman soldier in prison. While there, he wrote amazing letters to friends and groups of friends whom he treasured and wanted to help and encourage. In one of them he said, "I have learned to be content, in whatever circumstance I find myself." Written while chained to a soldier, unable to move about, sitting on the floor in a Roman prison! How is that for an evaluation of his circumstances? Contented whatever the circumstances, he wrote.

All I can say now is, "How rich we are!" Family, friends, circumstances, a sense of achievement, however small and insignificant, and a sense of peace because, as my farmer friend said those years back, we have God. I may not have been the largest or the most successful farmer, nor have I achieved any significant recognition or fame for any reason. So be it, fame and fortune do not always turn out to be quite what they are cracked up to be.

To return to my basic source of inspiration again, I record two quotes. One is what Jesus Christ said of a simple woman, "She did what she could." No more, no less, but it brought her fame, and comfort too as she faced uncalled-for criticism. The other is a quote from the Apostle Paul's writings, and the soundest bit of advice which has ever come my way: "Whatever your hand finds to do, do it with all your strength."

As a young man, I reveled in trials of strength and endurance; I sought them out. The challenges of manual work, of learning manual skills and trying to be a bit ahead in these areas, seemed to me to call for a response. Later in life, things changed and challenges of spirit and determination, of moral strength and endurance came my way unasked, and with much kindly help and support they were overcome, until we sailed into calmer waters. The wealth we have accumulated along the way, far more valuable to us than any financial savings or investments we might have but equally tangible, are our family, our friends, our farm and home, and peace with our God. All secure and invaluable.

20

GOING STRONG

"The Lord stood with me, and strengthened me."

2 Timothy 4:17

As the years increase there is always the danger of repeating oneself. Like a stuck recording. However, to make a point I will repeat this quote: "It is the outcome that matters, not the income." Which begs the question, "What is the outcome?"

When Anne and I were enjoying a five day visit to the amazing Luangwa Valley Game Reserve in Zambia some years back, we met a number of folk from other parts of the world including Cape Town, Gloucestershire in the U.K., and Dallas in Texas. It was very companionable and there was some teasing and leg pulling, especially when they discovered how long we had been married (about sixty years at that stage). All in good fun.

One meal time, it suddenly became serious when one of them asked, "What is the secret of a long marriage?"

Without any hesitation, previous discussion or thought about it, we both answered in unison, "Commitment!"

What they did not go on to ask, but might well have done was, "What is the outcome of commitment?"

To which question my answer would be: "Contentment."

Am I truly contented? That is really up to me, and in many ways, I can say yes, I am. To be appreciated, loved and supported with concern by family and friends is a reward in itself. But what about my work life and my modest achievements? I do remember the rather pointless and obvious remark that appeared on my school reports with boring regularity, but which Dad took seriously: "He could have done better." Of course I could, and looking at the years that have gone by and all I have been involved in and responsible for, it still applies. I am very aware of that.

Some years ago, a couple from the U.K. was staying with us. I had known them when I was a teenager; they had been then and are still very good and supportive friends. They were farmers, and their life experiences have been much like ours. One evening, my friend and I were remembering our past, recalling events and doings in our farming business and activities. Unknowingly, and with all the confidence of hindsight, we both kept repeating the phrase, "What I should have done was this, or that." All of a sudden, our two wives who had been silently listening to us, started to laugh. We were a bit shocked, as this had been a serious conversation. It was our oft-repeated remark that had caused their amusement.

"Of course you should have," they said. "But you didn't!"

The point was, we did what we thought right at the time.

To return to the subject of marriage, perhaps one of the mostly commonly made mistakes is doing things without consultation. If you are not sure, ask your wife what she thinks. If you are sure, you should still ask your wife. You may not be able to follow her reasoning, but often she has intuition, just common-or-garden gut feeling, about things. This I am saying for the men who are reading this book. I am sure it may be true for wives to consult with their husbands as well, but being a man, I cannot comment on that.

Often, I discussed with my son Brian how we would operate in partnership if we joined forces and had a farm big enough for the two of us. Anne was absolutely adamant that we should not do this; it just would not work, she said. No matter how we argued the point, she just knew. As it turned out, there was no opportunity for this to be, and we did not pursue it. We farmed independently, but in our own way we were able to support one another. I often asked his advice or help, and he mine. And how right that turned out to be.

People seem to have partners these days, not wives or husbands. They don't know what they are missing. But, and I emphasize this, our spouses should be our partners as well in every sense of the word. One of the joys of life is sharing things and experiences (that is why I have enjoyed writing this book). In a good marriage—marriage as it is meant to be—that is the greatest thing. The sharing should be in practical ways like joint Bank accounts, right through to confidences and unloading our fears or sorrows, our joys and expectations. I'm in danger of repeating myself again, but I dare to do that. We were married when we were young and irresponsible, with very little structure or security to support us. But we have never regretted it, not for one moment. We may have felt like murder, often, but divorce or just breaking up, never. In that sense I am contented, completely.

Enough of that. What do I do in my retirement? This question I have been asked a number of times.

For a start, I am writing these memoirs. It has been great, taking this journey, and it has been a journey. Many of the things and people I have written about are gone, the world I was raised in has vanished. Few folk around today know anything of that time, even of WW2; that's history. When I recently wrote to my brother of the market days of our youth and the personalities connected with them, he replied that those days are gone forever. True, the world has moved on. Much of what I saw and experienced when I first came to Africa has given way to the present. Some things which were of the past I grieve for; others I am glad they are no more.

I recently read in a favourite old book a gripping tale of the vanished past, wherein the writer made the following comment:

"It is a vanished world. No journey, save that of the memory, can bring it back now." I can identify with that, so I would love to share a sampling of those memories and experiences so that at least my grandchildren—if ever they do me the honour of thinking about me and reading these words—can understand a little of what made me like I am and something of my heritage, an understanding of which I sincerely hope I have been able to pass on to them.

Apart from writing, I am enjoying being relieved of at least some of the responsibilities which have been mine in the past. It has been seventy years since the year I started working on my father's farm to the day I officially retired. No longer do I need to plan each day ahead for twenty or more farm employees as well as for myself. I no longer feel a bit guilty in taking half an hour off during daylight hours to sit in my armchair and read or watch the TV. More than that, I can give time to some of the more important things in life, to family and friends, and things I never had time to do before (or perhaps even the inclination, I must admit).

There is the garden to maintain and our big old house, ridiculously large for two elderly folks, but with lots of room for visitors and family when they come. We love it and would hate to leave it. As a visitor said once, "It has character," which could be interpreted in many different ways. It may be a bit shabby in places; some window frames don't fit too well, the roof leaks a bit in heavy rain, there are cracks in some of the walls, and the termites (always with us in Africa) must be kept at bay. But so what? It is home!

Above all we are thankful. Thankful to be independent, to have one another, and so much else. The past is gone, but the memories and heaps more that the past has given us so richly, are still here. In the words of the greatest warrior and musician King that Israel ever had, "Goodness and mercy have followed me all the days of my life," and the future, whatever it brings, is secure.

CPSIA information can be obtained
at www.ICGtesting.com
Printed in the USA
BVHW03*1606160418
513520BV00005B/39/P